Counterpoints

Drawing by Saul Steinberg. © 1963 The New Yorker Magazine, Inc.

Rodney Needham

Counterpoints

University of California Press
Berkeley   Los Angeles   London

University of California Press
Berkeley and Los Angeles, California

University of California Press, Ltd.
London, England

© 1987 by
The Regents of the University of California

Printed in the United States of America

1 2 3 4 5 6 7 8 9

Library of Congress Cataloging-in-Publication Data

Needham, Rodney.
  Counterpoints.

  Bibliography: p.
  Includes index.
  1. Opposition, Theory of.   2. Polarity (Philosophy)
I. Title.
BC199.06N44   1987   160   86-19158
ISBN 0-520-05835-6 (alk. paper)

For C. D.

Contents

Figures and Tables

Scheme

Many things are known, as some are seen,
that is by Parallaxis,
or at some distance from their true and proper beings,
the superficial regard of things
having a different aspect
from their true and central Natures.

Sir Thomas Browne

The concept of opposition is one of the most antique in the history of disciplined thought, and it is to be discerned in the most disparate and far-separated forms of civilization. It appears to be a tested instrument of ratiocination, symbolism, and social order. The extreme simplicity of its binary structure, linking the fewest terms capable of sustaining a relation, has encouraged the presumption that it is a primary factor in ideation. Concomitantly, it has been taken for an elementary intellectual construct, and hence as basic to epistemology and systematic analysis. Aristotle formalized the logical uses of opposition, Ogden dissected its employment in English discourse, and French anthropologists have made it the subject of recondite theories.

xi

Opposition would thus seem to be a fundamental notion and thereby qualified to serve as a basic predicate in the interpretation of human experience and its most general modes of representation. Yet the more particular the characteristics attributed to it, and the more intense the scrutiny directed at its constitution, the less does it prove to have that steady integrity. Under analysis its apparent unity is dispersed among a variety of connections; its uses are largely contingent, and its operational value derives mainly from its ambiguous and accommodating nature. Opposition, by this revised account, is nonetheless a deep and consequential idea, only it is far from strict or incisive.

The concept is not formal but metaphorical; the metaphor represents an image; and the image is the product of a vectorial intuition of relative locations in space. The recognition of its peculiar character makes for further quandaries in the practice of comparativism, but at the same time it reveals mental proclivities that are of a kind with the concept they have fabricated. The search for an intrinsic form in the concept of opposition calls into question the minds of the theorists as much as the collective representations that they interpret; and in the study of dual symbolic classification, as a paradigm of oppositional structure, a like interest attaches to the subliminal impulsions that underlie the order in the social facts. In these respects the analysis of the concept of opposition permits an advance in the comprehension of human thought, its imagery, and its grounds.

R. N.

All Souls College, Oxford
Trinity Term, 1985

Acknowledgments

That I may publish
with the voice of thanksgiving . . . .
Psalms 26:7

This monograph was prepared at Oxford in the fall of 1984 and was written in Hilary Term, 1985, when the main part of the argument was delivered as lectures for the University. The great resources of the Bodleian Library, and the services of its staff, have been unfailing aids in the prosecution of the study. The work was written within All Souls College, to which I am deeply obligated for its munificent support and inspiration. As constantly as over many years past, I remain most grateful to J. S. G. Simmons, sometime Fellow and Librarian of All Souls, for invaluable scholarly advice and friendly interest.

I am profoundly indebted to Saul Steinberg for kindly allowing me to use his drawing as the frontispiece. It was

xiii

Acknowledgments

originally published as the front cover to *The New Yorker* of May 25, 1963, and I am obliged to The New Yorker Magazine, Inc., for their permission to reproduce it. The drawing has been included in Saul Steinberg, *The New World* (London: Hamish Hamilton, 1965). Photograph: © Bodleian Library, Oxford; shelfmark 17075 c. 88. An earlier version (1961), which has a special interest by virtue of what it does not include (cf. below, chap. 2), is to be seen in Harold Rosenberg, *Saul Steinberg* (New York: Alfred A. Knopf, 1978), p. 61.

Among individuals who have helped with their advice, and to whom I express my thanks, are A. R. V. Cooper, G. E. R. Lloyd, C. I. McMorran, I. K. McGilchrist, B. K. Matilal, and G. H. Treitel. Auditors at my Monday-morning lectures on opposition, and who encouraged me by their attendance and attention, included Axel Aubrun, Dominique Casajus, Craig Myers, Scott Phillips, and Anne de Sales.

Geoffrey Lloyd's splendid book *Polarity and Analogy* (Cambridge: At the University Press, 1966) has been a constant source and example.

One

Prospect

Worauf kann ich mich verlassen?

Wittgenstein

I

The concept of opposition—that is, the opposition of concepts—has been accorded a remarkable prominence in many kinds of discourse and analysis. The influence of what has been called structuralism, the defining mark of which is taken to be the establishment of oppositions, has played a special part in propagating the concept and has contributed also to the assumption that scientifically it has been well tested. It has been held to express a spontaneous and necessary act of the mind, such that it is to be found in every type of culture.

These supposed characteristics would seem to claim for

opposition a special value in attempts to arrive at a general understanding of social forms and human powers. The only way to attain this understanding is by the widest practice of comparativism, but the greater the differences among the linguistic traditions studied, the less can it be presumed that the words of our common discourse will be adequate to that task. Again and again it has been found that inquiries have been misdirected by an uncritical reliance on ordinary words, and that description, classification, or analysis has been subverted or frustrated because of defects in our instruments of thought. Concomitantly, therefore, the interpretation of alien concepts has made necessary a parallel elucidation of the words in our own language that we take to be equivalent, and these in their turn have usually turned out to be polysemous or otherwise imprecise. Under numerous aspects, then, the science of comparativism has uncovered an array of conceptual hazards, and increasingly the investigator has been compelled to echo Wittgenstein's urgent question (1969, sec. 508): "What can I rely on?"

There is no a priori method for answering this question. Whitehead has described as "pathetic" the desire of mankind to start from "an intellectual base which is clear, distinct, and certain" (1958:51). What we can instead rely on is to be decided, in the end, only by the outcome of a sequence of varied tests and against the largest possible extent of ethnographic evidences. These tests involve a sustained dialectic between the analysis of social facts and the critique of concepts. The conclusions are always provisional, and there is no reason to think that they will ever be conclusive to the point of unqualified reliability. Certain recent critiques have focused on the concepts of fact, value, class, force, reversal, alternation, and depiction (Needham

1983); and in each case, it has been argued, a more perspicuous view of the resources and flaws of the concept in question can be gained by means of a kind of empirical philosophy. To the extent that each such demonstration is conceded to make an acceptable proof, this critical procedure can be of radical assistance in securing a theoretical progress.

In the present instance the concept isolated for analysis is that of "opposition," together with a congeries of other lexical concepts that are significantly related to it. It is one of the oldest concepts in logic and epistemology, not the invention of a fashionable anthropology, and it has a long history of steady use in some of the most profound of speculations. It has indeed the appearance of an ultimate simplicity such as might be thought appropriate to a primary operation of thought and, hence, to a basic predicate in the analysis of representations, whether individual or collective. It implicates only two terms, and in this respect it can be seen as exemplifying the simplest possible form of relation. Whether the relation itself is equally simple is a separate issue, and the present monograph is devoted to that question.

Already, however, doubt has been cast on the supposed simplicity of opposition. Numerous modes of this relation (as the matter is commonly phrased) have been distinguished, and it has been asserted that "there is no logical means of determining which, if any, of the different modes can claim to be paradigmatic or the ultimate type of opposition" (Needham 1983:94). Analyses carried out in terms of opposition are therefore, it is contended, made correspondingly unreliable, and the concept itself is "intrinsically disputable" (p. 112).

II

There are many ways of presenting a critique of the concept of opposition, but one way that is out of the question is to try to make a complete coverage of its employment. The very fact that this ambition would be unrealizable is a testimony to the extraordinary hold of the notion, and it emphasizes also that merely to attempt to be reasonably comprehensive would not serve either. Tarde tried to do something of the kind in his ambitious work *L'Opposition universelle* (1897), but one of the most memorable lessons of method that it leaves in the mind is to resist what he called "the facile and disappointing charm of collecting antitheses" (p. v). A gloomier formulation is that of Lupasco, who has alluded to the "monotonous oscillation of antithetical dynamisms" (in Morel 1962: v). It is imperative, therefore, to avoid compiling a catalogue of examples and types, which would inevitably prove tedious, and to adopt some more concise style of exposition. Correspondingly, there can be no intention to report the views of all those who have published theoretical accounts of opposition; thus it is not to be held against the present argument that it could have taken into account certain psychological contentions (those of Jung would perhaps be the most obvious) or the structural pronouncements of any particular anthropologist, philosopher, mythologist, or student of comparative religion. The overriding concern must be to search for what, if anything, may be intrinsic to the concept of opposition, and the method adopted here has had that aim unremittingly in view. The argument, then, cuts a sequence of traverses across a very extensive and accidented terrain. The trails of many other investigators wind here and there, often crossing our own, but it is not our set task to compose a map or to write a history of exploration.

There are certain special features of the exposition that call for some preliminary comment. The first must be that the successive analyses that make up the chapters are demanding and frequently rather technical. In contrast with the postulated simplicity of the relation of opposition, the investigation encounters a proliferation of complexities, and the resolution of these calls for arduous attention. Whatever style of presentation may be chosen, the topic itself is intricate and perplexing, and the analysis necessarily reflects these characteristics. Despite the amusing allure of the frontispiece, the text is unavoidably rather forbidding and specialized; 'twill be caviare to the general.

III

The substantive case opens, not with ethnographic data, but with the genial drawing by Saul Steinberg. This is idiosyncratically attractive as a scheme for analysis, and it makes certain points of method as effectively as an ordinary anthropological example would do, but it also has two more consequential advantages. The first is that it displays the influence of opposition in a context in which it was not to be expected; the second is that the singularity of this artefact helps to prevent us taking anything for granted, as we might slip into doing if we were analyzing collective representations.

The next four chapters follow directly enough, and each in itself calls for no preparatory observations; but chapters 7 and 8 are likely to make a different impression, and some help may be called for in coming to terms with them.

It is not often in social anthropology that a complete change of theoretical direction is advocated, nor, for that matter, is it also contended that everything that has been done before is wholly mistaken. This however is the position adopted by Louis Dumont, with regard to the analysis of opposition and in particular of dual symbolic classification. A work on opposition that did not seriously examine this point of view would be defective theoretically, and it could also give the appearance of evading a scholarly challenge. Chapter 7, therefore, is a conscientious attempt to render an exact account of Dumont's opinions, very much in his own words, and then to assess their cogency. This is all very taxing, but it has to be done. For the most part, moreover, the argument is conducted in general terms that call for no prior knowledge, of a detailed factual kind, on the part of the reader.

But chapter 8 is another matter, and unless its presence and character are justified in advance it is quite likely to be found somewhat tedious. In fact, however, it is essential, and on more than one score, and it has to assume more or less the form in which it is presented. The main reason for this recourse is that the work by Tcherkézoff that is the subject of chapter 8 is based on the theory adumbrated by Dumont and examined in chapter 7; but whereas Dumont deals in generalities, Tcherkézoff criticizes a particular ethnographic test case. This is the very stuff of social anthropology, as an empirical discipline, and it is after all the only way to find out whether or not the theory advocated is correct. Ideally, of course, the reader should first go back to the sources, but even without that advantage the crucial facts are sufficiently reported, within the chapter itself, to allow an independent assessment of the points at issue. Another reason to treat this case in some detail is that it has to do with the analysis of a system of dual classification, which in turn is seen as constructed with opposites. Now opposition is represented as the simplest mode of relation, and dual classification can be seen as the systematic expression of that relation; in this respect, therefore, dual classification can be regarded as the ultimately simple institution. It may well be thought, in consequence, that if we cannot make sense of such elementary matters there is little chance of understanding more complex types of classification and more intricate aggregates of social facts.

It will be seen, all the same, that the analysis of a particular system of dual classification runs into many difficulties, and that not all of these are intrinsic to the subject matter. If it is thought that the issue, at one point or another, is being made altogether too difficult, it may be reassuring to recall what Wittgenstein has said (1967, sec. 452) about another kind of conceptual enterprise: "Philosophy unties knots in our thinking; hence its results must be simple, but philosophizing has to be as complicated as the knots it unties." Nevertheless, not everything about the investigation is complicated or problematical, and in one basic respect it is quite simple. There is an anthropological quip that there are two kinds of people in the world—those who divide everything into two and those who don't. Yet, for all the ingenious effect of this maxim, a recurrent implication of the various arguments deployed below is that actually there is only one kind and that everybody is inclined to think in twos. In more staid terms, there is an innate predisposition to order representations dyadically, even if there is much variation in the extent to which civilizations embody this tendency in their institutions. It is this simple factor that underlies the varieties of opposition. The subliminal formation of this factor itself is by definition obscure, but it is of very great interest.

Two

Explication

When acquiring knowledge we have sometimes to commence
not from what are logically the first principles of our subject,
but from the point whence we can learn most easily.

Aristotle

I

Saul Steinberg once drew for *The New Yorker* a cover that
typically combines the absurd with the enigmatic (see frontispiece). The central subject is a large capital E; from it
rise bubbles of thought or imagination toward a cartoonist's balloon containing another capital E. Also present in
the drawing are a dog and a cat, a hen with two chicks,
a potted plant, and a foreground of vegetation. What is
going on?

Let us start from the former E, taking it as indeed the
subject but without presuming that the significance of the
scheme is intrinsic to this letter alone. It is especially important that we take nothing for granted; but we have to

start somewhere, and the central E looks in fact as though it were intended as the subject, in a substantive sense at any rate, and thus to serve as starting-point. Of course, if we are to take nothing for granted, we do not want to make any presumptions about the artist's intentions either. So let us just say that the central component is the large E, more or less in the middle of things, and start from that. Yet in adopting this recourse we have already run the risk of taking something for granted, just by describing the letter as central. We can well say that it is geometrically central, as nearly as makes no matter, but this fact does not necessarily make it the semantic center. It may well turn out to be such, particularly since it is represented as a cerebrating subject, but even in that event it will not automatically, by that consideration alone, provide the key to the significance of the scheme as a whole. Not that we can presume, for that matter, that the scheme has in fact an integral significance, but that precisely is the question we are trying to answer.

Taken by itself, the large E is three-dimensional; it has bulk, and it rests on the earth. The shading on the surface toward the viewer, leaving out of account the partial hatching on other surfaces, makes the letter look rather gray or neutral in tone. It is certainly solid, for the cat is sitting on its bottom bar—on the assumption, of course, that the cat itself is supposed to be solid. That the E is upright, and that it is oriented from proper right to proper left, are attributes consistent with its character as a letter in the alphabet; but even these attributes are not to be taken for granted on that account, for Steinberg might well have conceived a motive for setting it at an angle or turning it backwards. It appears to be illuminated from above right (by stage or heraldic conventions) and somewhat from the front; light falling at an angle of about 130° would cast the shadows seen on the letter, though it does not itself project any shadow. The light and shade throw into relief the third dimension of the letter and give it an apparent solidity.

Let us next focus attention on the other E, above the former. Not that it is obviously the next component, as though it were next in importance or next in a direct connection. It is linked to the first E merely by two bubbles, whereas the cat is actually sitting on the letter and the dog is lying right in front of it and thus next to it in that sense. So we are not presuming a scale or line of significance when we look next at the upper E. Taken by itself, then, just as we took the former letter, this E has its own clear set of attributes. It is two-dimensional, it has no bulk, and it floats in the air. Concomitantly, it has no shading but is of an even black. It is upright, and it is oriented in the direction normal for this letter. It is marked with an acute accent. The balloon that frames it probably intimates that it is immaterial.

The other components in the drawing are quite naturalistically rendered; it is difficult to say anything interesting or revealing about their attributes, and there would be no obvious point in describing in equivalent words what is so patently represented in line. The dog looks straight out at the viewer, and so does the cat; the hen may be looking askance in the wary fashion of its species, but it is not head-on to the viewer. The dog is oriented to proper right, and so is the hen; the cat's body is oriented to the proper left. The potted plant is to the right (by the present conventions) of the lower E. The vegetation extends across the foreground; at the right edge there rises a flower-like growth.

Considered phenomenally, these are the components of the drawing and some of their distinctive attributes. That is about as far as we can go in such terms. If significant values inhere in the components, or if they are meant individually to connote additional meanings, nothing of the sort is at all evident. All we have achieved so far is a more particular registration of just what is where. That is not much of an answer to the question of what is going on.

II

Let us now look alternatively for an order in the drawing. This means analyzing it structurally, or in other words by isolating relations. Instead of trying to perceive the content of the components, we need to abstract the principles of order that articulate them. The principles may then enable us to infer something of the values that inspire the drawing, and thence permit an interpretation of its meaning.

We began by describing the central E as being linked to the upper one by rising bubbles of thought or imagination. The former letter is the active subject; the latter is an object in its consciousness. The figment (the accented E) is above that which has conceived it. No doubt this disposition agrees with the cartoonist's convention by which inner statements or ideas are placed within just such balloons above the heads of the characters depicted. Presumably, indeed, this is what Steinberg expects us to recognize. At the same time, however, the convention may indicate more than it represents; that is, it may provide an axis of explication that will pertain to the scheme as a whole. So let us be guided by this vertical dimension, and, in the course of considering the scheme under this aspect, try to make out the values of the components that are thus connected.

We shall begin again with the capital letters. The lower E

is expressly depicted as three-dimensional; it is massive and ponderous. The upper E is just as clearly drawn as two-dimensional; it is immaterial and weightless. Let us at this point adopt a convention in order to formulate such contrasts. The solidus, the oblique stroke ordinarily used in order to denote alternatives such as and/or, will serve the purpose. (An alternative possibility, as employed for instance in the *Oxford Dictionary of English Etymology* [Onions 1966:xii], is the sign)(which is to be read as "contrary to, the opposite of," but it is less simple and familiar, and it offers no overriding advantage.) The relation between the two letters can then be represented as three-dimensional/two-dimensional; massive/immaterial; ponderous/weightless. There are also, as we have seen, other phenomenal attributes that can similarly be contrasted: plain (unaccented)/accented; terrestrial/ethereal; neutral/definite (black). We can readily add: squat/slender; large/small (perhaps petite would be apt, though this is less of a phenomenal quality and may imply a prejudicial connotation). It has already been remarked that the bubbles and the balloon are conventional signs of what is thought or imagined, and this link supplies the contrasts: subject/figment; concrete/imaginary (taking this epithet to cover ratiocination as well). It would of course be possible to isolate further attributes as phenomenal contrasts; for example, the serifs of the lower E are squared off, whereas those on the upper E are inclined and tapered. But by this point in our survey we have run through those attributes that we listed individually as those of each letter, and this exercise has begun to elicit an order in the scheme. The principles of this order, so far as the analysis has been taken, are the vertical axis of explication and the linking along this dimension of an array of dyadic contrasts.

Let us see if these principles can also be said to articulate other components. The first candidates for assessment are the dog and the cat. The dog is lying on the ground, just as the lower E rests on the earth. The cat, if not ethereal, is in an airy position and is above the dog. It is plausible that they are to be taken as forming a set, giving the contrast dog/cat. The order in which these creatures are named in this dyad is dictated by the contrast below/above. This relation defines also the contrast between the hen and the chick on her back: hen/chick. (There is, of course, another chick; we shall come to that in a moment.) Finally we have the contrast between the rank, weed-like vegetation emerging from the earth and sprawling all over the foreground with the cultivated plant growing in the flowerpot, giving: untended/cultivated; vegetation/flower. Within this set, moreover, there can be posited yet another contrast, that between the flower rising from the vegetation, at proper right, and the blooms of the cultivated plant, yielding as a concluding contrast of a phenomenal kind: wild flower/ potted bloom. At this point we can therefore postulate that the two principles do indeed compose an order among these components as well as between the letters.

By this account, then, the vertical axis of explication and the dyadic constitution of sets of attributes are the principles of order that articulate the scheme. These principles, moreover, are formal, if in different senses, and in discerning them we have deliberately abjured nonformal inferences and the play of intuition. This method has enabled us to postulate a structure, or at least the grounds of such, for we certainly have not finished with the specification of what is here articulated into a structure. Before we pass on to that task, however, we ought to take a skeptical look at the principles themselves.

First, the axis of explication. This is given by the relative locations of the two letters, on the assumption, that is, that these are crucial to the definition of the scheme. This is a fair assumption, for reasons we have adduced, and it is confirmed by the apparent absence of an alternative dimension of explication. Indeed, it is remarkable, in a comparative perspective, that lateral discriminations (right/left) come so little into play. The dog and the cat are turned toward proper right, as are the chicks; the potted plant and the wild flower are to the right of the lower E; the cat's body is turned to the left. There is no sign here of a formal symmetry of dispositions or of a significant balance of the contrasted components by reference to the sides. And as for some other axis in relation to which an order might be established, there is even less sign of that.

The other principle, that of dyadic contrast, is more contestable. This also is given by the two letters; first by the fact that there are two of them, and then by the relative locations that propose the contrast below/above as an axis of explication. But the other contrasts are not quite so patent as this. The dog and the cat form a conventional pair as domestic animals, and also in the common saying about fighting like cats and dogs. They are not the only creatures in the drawing, however; there are also the hen and her chicks, and it is a question why these should not be aggregated with the dog and the cat. We have taken it that the hen and the chick on her back qualify as a distinct set because they form a pair, and because as such they qualify by the contrast below/above. Yet there is a second chick, on the ground behind the hen, and the presence and position of this creature are not accounted for by our principles. It is moreover a third representative of the species, and this leads to the point that the number of species represented (dog, cat, fowl) is also three. Does this mean that another principle, that of the triad, has to be recognized? Well, it cannot be adopted in the explication of the rest of the scheme, for there are only two letters, only two kinds of vegetable growth, only two kinds of flower. So if it were admitted it would still not serve as a principle of the kind we set out to seek, namely, such as would operate as a general mode of articulation throughout the scheme. In other words, the triad does not pertain to the structure. Whether the two triads have an ancillary part to play in the significance of the drawing is a question that we shall be in a position to assess when we examine the possibility of inferring the values that may inspire it.

III

We have now identified the components of the drawing and have registered their distinctive attributes; we have abstracted the principles that articulate them; and to a point we have justified the principles. Taking the drawing as a formal scheme, we have discerned a structure in it.

But the components are not formal representations; they are depicted as empirical realities, and, whether taken singly or in combination, they are resonant with possible values. These values are among those of western civilization, and we ought therefore to be able to appreciate them. This may not be possible to a pitch of utter certainty, but we ought to be capable of working out a general pattern of significance that will be more than just plausible. In order to do this it will be useful to represent what we have learned by a means that will enable us to comprehend it as a whole. In particular, the contrasts need to be considered in a single frame. So far, we have considered them, for the most part, in no more than a cumulative fashion, and we have had to hold in our heads the occasional associations and distinctions among them that have been suggested. To represent them on the line—below/above, terrestrial/ethereal, and so on—would bring them together, and it might prompt a recapitulation of certain points of comparison, but it would hardly serve very well to display an order among them.

A ready means of doing this was attributed by Aristotle, in the *Metaphysics,* to certain Pythagoreans and can be dated therefore back to the fifth or perhaps the sixth century B.C. They maintained, he said, that there were ten first principles "arranged in parallel columns" (trans. Warrington 1961:65; see present table I). The method is thus peculiar to literate civilizations, a point that will find its relevance later. For the present, let us merely take note of the point, and emphasize that the method was the invention of metaphysical philosophers. It is conceivable that a scheme of contrasts might be represented in nonliterate societies by

TABLE I
Pythagorean Principles

limited	unlimited
odd	even
one	plurality
right	left
male	female
at rest	in motion
straight	crooked
light	darkness
good	evil
square	oblong

material mnemonics, in the form of various objects or perhaps even by differing scratches on the ground, but for the
present this is a possibility that we can set aside. The Pythagorean principles, anyway, were defined by contrasts
such as limited/unlimited, odd/even, one/plurality, and so
on; and these, according to Aristotle, were arranged in two
columns: limited, odd, one, . . . in one column, and un-
limited, even, plurality, . . . in the parallel column. This
means of representing a dualistic conception of things is
thus quite antique, and it has a long history of use down to
our own day. It is a standard resource in the expositions of
historians of ideas and philosophers, and it has acquired a
special vogue among anthropologists. It has also attracted
criticism, and on counts that might seem to deprive it of
much of its apparent usefulness: we shall deal with these
contentious matters in due course. Let us for the present
adopt the table of opposites as a method of representation
and see what use can be made of it.

The contrasts extracted from the drawing are, then, to
be arranged in two parallel columns. It will be remembered
that we want to take nothing for granted; the arbitrary and
the tendentious are equally to be avoided. Nevertheless, before we can even begin to draw up the two columns a decision has to be taken. Which terms are to go into which column? In isolating the contrasts, we have put the terms of
each into an order. This order was provided by the choice
of the lower E as the central component and as the subject
of the drawing, and then, taking this letter as the starting
point, by the vertical axis of explication. So the contrast
corresponding to the axis was set down in the order in
which the lower E was compared with the upper E; that is,
as below/above. Afterwards this order was tacitly maintained, so that what was below was treated first and then its

counterpart above; for example, dog/cat. This order was pragmatically determined and was not meant to express any relative evaluation of the terms composing a contrast; there was no implication, that is, that the term set down first was to be ranked as first in any other respect. This methodical detachment accorded with the formal nature of our analysis of the scheme; we identified the components but did not ascribe any content to them, and similarly we registered the contrasts without assuming that the relation implied a difference in value between the two terms. So just as below/above is formally equivalent to above/below, it might be thought that it should make no difference which terms were listed in each of the proposed columns. Yet that is not what is taught by the actual employment of the method. The Pythagoreans reported by Aristotle placed "right" in the column to proper right, and "left" in the column to proper left; male, straight, light, and good were in the right column, and female, crooked, darkness, and evil were in the column of the left. When read in Greek or English, the first term in each contrast appears to be superior in some respect or another to the second term, as these are encountered on the line. This example has had numerous successors, especially in the practice of anthropologists, and it has become a standard expectation that an arrangement in two columns is meant to be read as expressing contrasts not only in terms but also in values. It is not a matter of indifference, therefore, whether we write below/above or above/below, and so on.

We can either fall in with this implicit convention, even if we find that in our present case we have to reject what it implies, or else we can adopt the alternative arrangement and try to avert misunderstanding by stating the reason for doing so. One possible reason for the latter course is that it replicates the order provided by the axis of explication. This is not merely a notional line; it is a vector, and the attention is carried along it from below to above. But the direction of this vector is not intrinsic to the scheme; it is a consequence of our premise that the lower E is the subject of the drawing, and of our decision to start the analysis from it. Formally speaking, however, it would have been equally valid to start instead from the upper E; the vector of explication would then have gone in the opposite direction, above/below, and all of the subsequent contrasts could have been established equally well in this sense. Our first principle, therefore, does not determine the constitution of the two columns. Another reason to retain the order to which we have so far resorted is that we have in fact resorted to it, and that it would simply be inconsistent or untidy to switch direction when we came to sum up the results in two columns. This recourse has an appeal that is itself orderly, but since the order in the analysis is pragmatic, not intrinsic, it does not provide decisive grounds for adopting an expository arrangement of the same nature. Indeed, these considerations suggest a reason for not retaining the order of the opening analysis.

To transpose the terms that make up the contrasts would emphasize their character as formal constructs, and would restate the premise that the order in which they are registered is intended to carry no significance. If the terms prove to have contrastive values, these will be evident whichever of the two arrangements we adopt. If there turns out to be a general weighting in favor of one column, in comparison with the other, it will be pointless or perverse to assign it to the proper left. If there is no such general disparity in values between the two columns, there is nothing to be lost by following the convention; for the demonstration of equality will then be carried out by reference to the arrangement reflecting what seems at first to be a disparity.

IV

An appropriate arrangement of the terms is suggested by the connection between the two letters. The bubbles intimate thought or imagination, but not precisely what is in the head of the lower E. Here we have to start making inferences about content.

It looks as though the lower letter is dreaming about the upper, or perhaps forming an image of an ideal E. A plausible construction is that the heavy earthbound E is longing for the qualities of the light ethereal E. There are many ways of phrasing this state of mind, but we do not want to ascribe too many particulars to whatever occupies the mind of the subject of the drawing. For the moment, the object is to make a reasoned decision about the arrangement in which the contrasts shall be presented. The upper E is not only above the other letter, but, on the suggested premise, it is superior to it in other respects as well. Even this rather vague qualification will assign it to what by convention is generally the superior column; that is, the one to the proper right. From this starting point we can then arrange the other contrasts as in table 2.

There is nothing contrived about this table; it is simply a pragmatic list. The contrasts have been entered in the order in which they were encountered in section II above, and the allocation of terms to one or the other of the columns has been explained. Yet, to the extent that this consolidation of our findings permits a clearer view of their import, the table also suggests further connotations. These are not

TABLE 2
Phenomenal Attributes

upper E	lower E
above	below
ethereal	terrestrial
two-dimensional	three-dimensional
slender	squat
light	ponderous
accented	plain
imaginary	concrete
cat	dog
chick	hen
flower	weed
cultivated	untended
potted bloom	wild flower

given phenomenally; they are inferred from the values that are commonly ascribed in other contexts to the entities depicted. To begin with, the cartoonist's convention has led us to conceive that the lower E in some regard aspires after the condition of the upper E. The qualities attributed to the two letters respectively include the contrast heavy/light, but also, we can reasonably add, clumsy/graceful (reversed, of course, when entered in the table). It would be easy to find other epithets that would similarly fit the kind of contrast that we see. What is more interesting is the possibility of expanding the scope of the contrast by linking such evaluative connotations to further attributes of other terms.

The cat and the dog are contrasted not only as species and by their respective locations but also by conventional qualities and associations. These are collective representations, in other words, but of course a great deal depends on the particular collectivity whose values we choose to cite: there are fundamental esthetic differences, and perhaps incompatibilities of temperament as well, between cat-lovers and dog-lovers. So let us say merely that there is a body of conventional support for regarding the cat as graceful and subtle by comparison with the relative clumsiness and bluffness of the dog. A similar contrast is commonly drawn, and perhaps with less division of opinion, between the appealing helplessness of the chicks and the fairly exasperating fussiness of the hen. They can also readily be contrasted as: young/old, innocence/experience, expectation/resignation, and so on. Finally, the plant and vegetation suggest further evaluations. The cultivated bloom stands precisely for cultivation and care, by contrast with the coarseness and neglect conveyed by the rank vegetation. Even the potted bloom and the wild flower, which are not that different to look at, carry the contrasted evaluations of disciplined/unrestrained. It is no more than exact, though implying much else besides, to say that here we see emblematized the contrast culture/nature.

We have thus been carried again through the drawing, and down the lines of table 2, and we have accumulated by inference an additional array of contrasts, only this time expressing contrastive values. These can be represented together as in table 3. There is an interesting agreement of general import between these two representations of the scheme under analysis. Table 2, which is based on the formal principles of vertical explication and dyadic contrast, accords in a number of respects with table 3, which is based instead on imputed values. To an extent, of course, some agreement is only to be expected, for the values are those ordinarily ascribed to the terms or objects of table 2,

TABLE 3
Evaluative Connotations

ideal	reality
graceful	clumsy
subtlety	bluffness
appealing	exasperating
helplessness	fussiness
young	old
innocence	experience
expectation	resignation
cultivation	coarseness
care	neglect
disciplined	unrestrained
culture	nature

and they therefore replicate the order of the latter. Nevertheless, it is not for this reason alone that there is a general concordance between the phenomenal and the evaluative. The clear implication is that the principles and the values, as also the agreements between them, express a character that is intrinsic to the drawing. This character is the significance imparted by the artist to his invention; the order discerned by analysis is the meaning of the drawing.

Presumably, therefore, Steinberg had that order in mind when he conceived the scheme. With some degree of deliberation, he must, by this account, have formulated the principles that we have isolated, and he must have assessed the values that we have inferred. It is not necessary, however, that he should have done so with complete detachment, for in constructing one part or another of his drawing, as in its original conception (cf. the earlier version mentioned in the Acknowledgments), he could well have been guided in part by his subconscious. No doubt this source of significance is stocked with collective representations, both cultural constituents and principles of order, but these alone are by no means the only subliminal factors that could have been responsible for the structural significance of Steinberg's drawing.

Three

Precisions

All our words,
especially those in which are contained
general and universal ideas,
are each like a little chaos.

Swedenborg

I

The analysis carried out in the preceding chapter was not pushed to extremes, and many possible alternatives and qualifications were left out of account; also, numerous questions could have been asked about how one assesses the general import of a table in two columns of contrasts. The considerations actually adduced were merely some of the essential preliminaries to the investigation of fundamental modes of thought and imagination. The chapter was, in other words, a reconnaissance.

Yet all the same the analysis may well have seemed intricate enough, and especially in view of the relative simplicity of the case. We were dealing with a scheme composed of only ten entities, and we explicated its structure by reference to only two principles; one of these principles is a single vector, and the other is dyadic and thus formally the simplest mode of relation. So, if even a preliminary analysis need be complicated to the pitch we have determined, there is an obvious inference to be drawn. This is that the apparent simplicity of the dualistic scheme conceals a combination of factors that do not possess this simplicity. Some of these factors may be intrinsic to the construction of the scheme itself; others may have to do with the concepts and the frame of mind with which we apprehend the scheme. There is the possibility, moreover, that part of the intricacy of the matter is the product of factors that are common both to the constructor of the scheme and to the analyst. This range of factors may be individual or collective, and they may be deliberate or subliminal. No wonder, therefore, that the analysis uncovers one complication after another, and also that there are queries, qualifications, and decisions about method that have to be held in mind.

This state of affairs is expressed in the variety of words used to describe what we have here called contrasts. This word was chosen for its relative neutrality, in order not to import into the analysis the prejudicial connotations of one or another of the alternative words. Taken literally, by its etymology, "contrast" expresses the idea of "to stand (over) against"; as a verb, in its intransitive mode, it means to exhibit striking differences in a comparison. In the present instance, these senses have been qualified as dyadic, so that one term (thing, attribute) is taken to be contrasted with only one other comparable term. These are pretty minimal and designedly noncommittal premises; even if it has not yet been precisely stipulated what is to be understood by equivalents such as "to stand against," at least they convey the idea of significant difference in a direct comparison; and the qualification that the contrasts are dyadic means that the comparison is restricted to the minimal number of things to be compared.

The alternative means of describing the contrasts are words that have their own distinct derivations and histories of characteristic usage. They include antitheses, contraries, contrarieties, counterparts, counterpoints, dualities, dyads, oppositions, polarities, and syzygies. It will be worthwhile to scan the main words in this list in order to gain a general view of the sort of conceptual field that we are entering. It is already remarkable that any thesaurus should place at our disposal such a proliferation of more or less equivalent words, to which no doubt others could yet be added, so that at once we are given the impression of an essential unity that is differentiated accidentally or to special ends. But at the same time the various words incline us to wonder if they are really so much alike, and, if they are, why there are so many of them.

Some of the differences have to do with the classical language, either Greek or Latin, from which they come; others reflect more particular formations. The following will serve as examples. The word "antithesis" comes from the Greek for "to set or place against or opposite"; "contrary," from the Latin *contrā*, against or opposite; "counterpart" also comes from *contrā*, with the additional connotations of reversal, parallelism, or reciprocation, combined with "part" as a share or portion of a whole; "duality" is from the Latin for two, just as is "dyad," both being traceable to Greek; "opposition" is derived from Lat. *ob-*, towards, against, in the way of, and *pōnere*, to place; "polarity" is based on "pole" (Lat. *polus,* end of an axis), each of the two

27

PRECISIONS

opposite points on a celestial sphere, the earth's axis, or the surface of a magnet; "syzygy" is from the Greek for yoke, pair, copulation, conjunction.

It would be possible, though a lengthy business, to make a methodical comparison among all the alternatives to the noun "contrast" listed above, and to display the overlaps and distances among their several meanings. But by now the chief purpose of adducing them has been attained. There is no essential feature that unites them all, and they cannot be employed as synonyms one for another. They have more or less distinct denotations, and the use of each is appropriate to some subjects or contexts but not to others. These conclusions are readily justifiable by recourse to common English usage, as well as by reference to the roots and derivations of the words compared. Rather than sharing an intrinsic and distinct meaning, these words make up a polythetic conceptual class (see Needham 1983, chap. 2); that is, a set aggregated by serial or sporadic resemblances.

Nevertheless, there is one word among them that is preponderant, namely "opposition." In its components it is equivalent to "antithesis"; it forms part of the definition of the words formed on contra- and counter-; and it is implicit in "polarity" and to some extent in "syzygy." If we are looking for a general-purpose word that will serve to indicate the kind of relation underlying the contrasts we have isolated, and that will also intimate connections with the alternative words just treated, "opposition" will serve well enough. It is also very convenient, in that it is the word most commonly employed by anthropologists and students of comparative religion in the examination of dual symbolic classification, exotic cosmologies, and like topics. Of course, this familiarity also has its dangers, for it may give the impression that we know exactly what we are talking about when we speak of opposition; but we need to start at least by concentrating on a single lexical concept, rather than constantly survey a range of alternatives, and for this purpose the most comprehensive word offers the most advantages.

We shall focus, then, on opposition as the mode of relation; and also, naturally, on "opposite" as the adjective designating the relation, as well as that which stands in opposition. We have not yet established, though, what the meanings of these words are. The *Oxford English Dictionary* defines "opposition" as "position over against something," and the adjective as "placed or lying over against something on the other side or farther side of an intervening line, sphere, or thing; contrary in position." The meaning of the crucial words "over against," however, is "opposite" (Onions 1966 s.v.), so in this respect the definition is a tautology. "Against" is formed on "again," meaning in Old English "in the opposite direction" and derived from Common Germanic *ʒaʒan, direct, straight (cf. OE ġeġn, straight). The Germanic base *ʒaʒ is of unknown origin. Both definitions and etymology therefore leave us without a clear account of what is at issue, and for the present we must rely on common usage and lexical equivalents.

II

Our main purpose, it will be recalled, is to contribute to the search for basic predicates in the comparative analysis of social facts. If opposition is to qualify, it will need to be demonstrated as a propensity of the human mind or else as a conceptual necessity in coming to terms with representations.

A ready indication of its character, under either of these aspects, is to be looked for in the testimony of other languages. If it is truly basic, it can be expected to find recognition in any tongue. It is not necessary that it shall be expressed by only a single word, for periphrase could serve to identify the relation, but the likelihood seems to be that a basic predicate will be declared in a direct and economical form. Nor is it necessary that the mode of relation shall be abstracted by means of a lexical substantive, for an adjective equivalent to "opposite" would be sufficient evidence for a pragmatic recognition of the relation. That is, it should be sufficient that there be an equivalent to what the compiler of the dictionary understood by the English word "opposite." As for the sheer number of languages that would need to be consulted in order to provide a decisive proof, this is at present largely a matter of expository practicality. At the limit it would mean inspecting each of thousands of languages, and in each case it would be necessary also to make a contextual analysis of the word or words in question, to make sure that its equivalent to "opposite" really was equivalent—but this would call for a prior stipulation of those very features that we are seeking to establish. Faced with this situation, we shall opt for a summary assessment followed by a few selected instances.

We can start with the simple report that the ransacking of many dictionaries of exotic languages discovers just as many translations of "opposite," to the wearisome point indeed at which it strikes one that the quest ought really to be for a language in which no such recognition of opposition was to be found. This does not prove as much as it would seem to do, however, even with the precautions suggested above. A comparable search of dictionaries for equivalents of "belief" discovers numerous instances, but there is the gravest doubt that any of them, outside our own linguistic tradition, has the slightest claim to acceptance as evidence for a general recognition of what is denoted by the English word (Needham 1972). There is an obvious difference between the two cases, of course, in that "opposite" can be referred to a phenomenal perception of objects, whereas "belief" is supposed to be some sort of inner state, but the counter-example of the latter word nevertheless makes a salutary point about apparent equivalents in dictionaries. It may well be accepted that all languages make provision for the predicate of opposition, but we shall not know what this assumed fact is worth until we have gained, by the analysis of particular instances, a clearer idea of alternative linguistic means—if there are such—of stating the relation.

Within the Indo-European family, the Romance languages do not make a sufficient contrast, since their equivalents also derive from the Latin for "to place something over against something else." German is more interesting, in that the substantive *Gegenteil* appears to have referred originally to a social confrontation. It is derived from MHG *gegenteil,* meaning an opposing party in a legal dispute (Grebe 1963:705 s.v. Teil); but the crucial *gegen,* against, is of unknown origin (p. 203 s.v.; see above, sec. I, on "against"). This does not carry us very far, but it does at least indicate that in the formation of a word, or in the apprehension of a relation, different settings can be called upon to supply the illustrative context or what may have been the paradigmatic sense.

Sanskrit exemplifies a great civilization whose language is the instrument of an acutely self-conscious and philosophical tradition. The equivalent to "opposite," nevertheless, is direct and simple, reflecting none of the classificatory obsession or the logical ingenuity elsewhere characteristic of traditional Indian thought. The adjective *pratipākṣa* is a compound of *prati,* face to face, with *pākṣa,* side. The relation of opposition is also recognized, as we might have expected: the substantive *pratipākṣa-bhāva* denotes the state of being, *bhāva,* of the condition or position referred to.

In Egyptian, the language of another great and literate civilization, there were a number of words expressing opposition. The hieroglyphs transliterated as *mₑk3* meant opposite, to be opposite someone; also, significantly, (to shoot) at someone (Erman and Grapow 1925, 1:233). The characters *ḥsj* meant in opposition to, against (in the contexts of coming, jubilation, or standing firm in battle) (1929, 3:159).

In the Austronesian languages it is easy to find dictionary equivalents for "opposite," such as the Malay *tentang;* but the materials are lacking for a plausible reconstruction of their derivation, and an examination of usage, for example that of *tentang,* shows many agreements in sense but nothing about the formation of the word or words in question. This etymological block hinders the investigation of practically all exotic languages, for that matter; but Chinese, by virtue of the principles and antiquity of its script, proffers a glimpse of a truly distinct treatment of opposition.

In modern Chinese, to begin with, the character 對 which is conventionally spelt out as *tui*[4] or *duey* has the meanings of: opposite; to face, facing; towards; correct; (to) pair; to suit; to reply (Simon 1947:150 s.v. *duey*); it is the initial character in compounds meaning symmetry, opposite, to exchange, facing, to contrast, diagonal, antithetical, couplets, to confront (pp. 150–51). Another modern expression is *hsiang*[1] *tui*[4] or *shiang duey,* also meaning "opposite," in which the former character (radical 109, eye) means "mutual"; when combined alternatively to make *shiangfaan*, it again means contrary, opposite, vice versa (pp. 625–26 s.v. *shiang*); *faan* (rad. 29, also, again) itself has the senses of to turn over, to turn back, to rebel, contrary, opposite (p. 167 s.v.). Here, then, we have from a literate and superbly sophisticated civilization, with a language etymologically quite unconnected with our own, the discrimination of a congeries of relationships including opposition; this relation is denoted not only by *duey* but by other characters as well.

The character now rendered phonetically as *duey* is ancient, and its senses include: answer a superior, respond; correspond, match, make a pair; symmetrical, proportionate, answering, correct; be opposite to, vis-à-vis, in front of; oppose, opponent (Karlgren 1923:323, char. 1140). Its archaic meanings are traced as: respond, in response; reply; correspond to, suitable; counterpart (Karlgren 1964:139, 141, char. 511). There are two main kinds of setting to be made out among this array of interconnected senses: one is a social confrontation, as in answering or opposing; the other is formal, as in matching or in making a pair, as also in the recognition of symmetry or a counterpart.

The constituents of the character have a special interest as possible indications of the archaic conception of the idea, though the reconstruction is difficult and uncertain. According to the advice of modern authorities, the following points have at any rate to be taken into account as possible factors in the interpretation of *duey*. To begin with, the character is classed in modern dictionaries under radical 41, inch, very small. This might seem to suggest the generic idea of measurement, which could seem apt to the spatial aspect of opposition. But in fact the radical is only a version of radical 64, a hand (cf. Karlgren 1923:316, char.

1113). The other part of the character presents real difficulty. It appears to be constituted on the basis of a character that was one of the 540 radicals employed by the *Shuo-wen,* compiled about A.D. 100, but what was then the meaning of that character is unsure; contemporary explanations were that it meant densely growing grass or vegetation, and also emerging side by side. However, an attractive recent proposal (as yet unpublished) is that the nonradical part of *duey* represents a bouquet, so that the character as a whole depicts a hand holding a bunch of flowers. There are very many versions of it on the Chou bronzes, almost always in phrases expressing loyal gratitude to the king for his benevolence. It may have been metaphorical for flowery speech, and hence, it is suggested, by honorific use it came to mean "facing" or "confronting." It must be for sinologists to evaluate this reconstruction, but, to the extent that it is at least plausible, it provides a further clue to the formation of the concept of opposition. As could well have been expected (cf. Needham 1974:63–64), for the Chinese the paradigmatic sense was apparently social; and it seems also to have been imagined in a hierarchical setting, whether in paying compliments to a ruler or, more generally, in responding to a superior. An obvious inference, whether or not it is testable, is that the dispositions of the social setting came first, and that the relation of opposition was abstracted afterwards.

We have dwelt on the Chinese case at some length because of its distinct quality, its intrinsic interest, and its antiquity as recorded in evidences dating back well over two thousand years. But for all its power of instruction it is nevertheless just one instance, among myriad other testimonies, of the linguistic registration of opposition. There is no need to rehearse the cautions with which we began this section before we conclude that opposition seems to be universally recognized. Being so enregistered in language, it is imposed on the individual consciousness.

III

The seeming universality of the concept of opposition takes us back to a question that we raised but have not yet treated.

The concept may express a natural propensity of human thought, and the linguistic evidences can be interpreted in that sense. But we have also alluded to another possibility, namely that the concept may respond to an intellectual necessity in coming to terms with representations. In other words, if men are to take reliable account of their positions physically in relation to one another, or if they are to be able to describe the disposition of material objects in relation to one another, they may stand in absolute need of the idea of opposition. It would thus be one of what Cassirer called "the basic relations which constitute the unity of consciousness" (1953:94; cf. 198–215). This kind of impulsion, seen as an unevadable response of consciousness to its environment (which is not Cassirer's own view, by the way), need not be an alternative to the postulated propensity (which, in general, Cassirer did subscribe to), but it could operate conjointly with it. This premise naturally makes it hard to determine whether either factor, external or internal, is responsible for the apperception of opposition, or whether this is the product of both together. From a probative point of view, it might be thought most satisfactory if it were demonstrated that the propensity was matched and confirmed by the pragmatic necessity. We shall take up the question of empirical causation later in the argument. For the present it is the logical aspect, which is entirely general, that is at issue.

How can it be proved that opposition is an intellectual necessity? Not by comparative considerations, evidently, but, if it is at all possible, from first principles. We cannot presume that it will be feasible to do this, but we have to try. We can take as given, to begin with, that the capacity to make spatial differentiations of location, relative direction, and distance is a prerequisite for coping with the material environment, including, of course, other human bodies. In the present instance we are considering the matter of direction, whether of something relative to the viewer or else of a thing relative to some other thing. Let us start with the former of these two cases, as perhaps the easier in that we can put ourselves in the position of the subject who judges whether or not a thing is opposite himself.

A familiar setting is that of eating with others at table; let us assume that the table is oblong, with straight sides, as in a college hall. If those seated at table are as usual equally spaced, from the head of the table down, each person will have another sitting opposite. No explanation of what this means is necessary to anyone who understands the English language. The situation can be represented by a simple diagram (figure 1) of the coordinates of opposition. In this figure, V stands for the viewer; R is the viewer's right, L is left; O is whatever is opposite the viewer. The angle of view is stipulated as a right angle (90°) because if something is to be opposite it must be right in front of the viewer, straight ahead; what these expressions mean is determined by the lateral base line R—L. It is this implicit paradigm that is departed from when someone says that

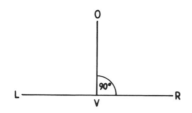

Figure 1. Coordinates of Opposition

something is "almost opposite" or "nearly opposite" something else. If someone does not turn up for dinner, and the place setting and chair reserved for that person are removed, the other diners on that side of the table will be spaced out (equally, let us assume) in order to fill the gap. How far they will move, to one side or the other, will depend on how many they are; if they are few the distance will be relatively considerable, if they are many it will be less noticeable. In either event, at what extent of displacement will it then be said that a given viewer no longer has another diner opposite? The actual effect of our example would depend not only, as we have remarked, on the number seated along one side of the table but also on the width of the table; the wider it is, the smaller will be the angle subtended by any given lateral displacement. (An accurate assessment calls for this much detail; otherwise the case cannot be made.) What we need to formulate, therefore, is a general rule by which to estimate whether or not a diner on the other side of the table is opposite (O) the viewer (V). Strictly speaking, any deviance from the right angle would mean that the person on the other side was not opposite, so that an angle on the right of 89° would be a disqualification. Can the rule be formulated, then, by the angle of deviance, in this instance only one degree? Or is there a pragmatic latitude on either side and within which the description "opposite" will still be correct or at any rate admissible?

Well, we do qualify the adjective positively as though the strict opposite might be departed from without invalidating the description. We say, namely, that something is exactly opposite, or dead opposite, or directly opposite, and so on. But it is a question how such phrases are to be analyzed. The qualifier may be no more than an intensifier, a gloss that, properly speaking, is redundant but that emphasizes the information that whatever is in question is indeed opposite, and not, for example, almost opposite or within an indeterminate extent such as the opposite side of a street. By this reading of the situation, no latitude is implied: dead opposite means opposite. On the other hand, also, people are usually careful about declaring a deviance from the opposite; it is standard usage to qualify the location of something as being almost opposite, practically opposite, not quite opposite, and so on. These various indications combine to give the strong impression that actually no discernible latitude is allowed for: opposite should mean opposite. It is not a question of reckoning an acceptable angle of deviance; if any deviance at all is detected, a qualifier will at once be brought into play, so that the object is said to be not quite opposite or at most to be as good as opposite. These phrases also work against the idea that to say "exactly opposite" implies the admissibility of an opposite that is not exact.

So these facts of common usage, in the English language, serve to show that no detectable deviance is permitted to count as "opposite." There is no special factor at work, such as pedantry or a superior command of idiom or a good eye for angles. These expressions are the common means of giving directions and specifying locations. In the case of our present example of the dinner table, in particular, there is ordinarily no matter of etiquette at stake, either, so it is not this that makes us so punctilious in the assessment of opposition. Yet, it seems, something does.

IV

The issue is so radical, as well as causally obscure, that a quick glance at some other examples may be helpful.

We speak of the opposite side of a street, which may sound as though an enormous extent of deviance were admitted; but it means no more than that for any point on this side of the street there is a point on the other side that is opposite. It certainly does not mean that, for any point on this side, any point whatever on the other side is opposite to it. We speak also of the opposite bank of a river, which is an interesting case in that the course of a river is usually winding, so that a series of curves is correlated with other curves that may be various in form and at differing distances. In this case, any given point is located on a notional base line between nearby points upstream and downstream from it, and it is from this base that the point is opposite a single point on the opposite bank. On an outside bend, too, a number of successive points may have lines of opposition that cross in mid-water, so that their opposites on the other bank are in inverse order.

Finally, let us mention the treatment of solid objects. A cube, such as a tea container, seen from one side, has an opposite side; neither side, as an exterior surface, faces the other, yet they are said to be opposite from the point of observation of the viewer. In such a case the flat sides do not introduce the question of deviance, but the matter is not so clear in the case of a cylindrical container such as a can for baked beans. With this, there is strictly speaking no discrete side but instead the visible portion of a continuous curve. Nevertheless, this facing surface is spoken of as a side, and it actually has an opposite side. This is a notional and relative surface, not of course one given by the conformation of the object; it is defined by reference to a line projected from the viewer through the middle of the visible surface, and diametrically through the center of the can, to an opposite point on the invisible and converse curve. All the same, there is no falling off in the careful accuracy with which it is said that a particular point, say an emblem or a letter on the label, is opposite some other mark on the far side of the cylinder. It is not an obsession with solid geometry that is at work here, but the compulsion of linguistic usage.

There is something particularly striking about this usage. In the ordinary way, "words strain, crack and sometimes break . . . , decay with imprecision, will not stay in place," yet in the case of "opposite" the word seems to have retained a rigid precision. If it is suspected that the verb "retained" begs the question, since we have no evidence that "opposite" was employed with equal strictness in past centuries, there are at least two responses to be made. In the first place there are the etymological connotations of straightness or directness. In the second, it is most improbable that a previous laxity in the denotation of "opposite" should have become disciplined, in ordinary discourse, into the present exactitude; that is not the way words work. The normal effect of constant use is the enlargement of sense, the admission of further criteria, and a less direct connection with the formative or paradigmatic meaning. Yet the adjective "opposite" is used with strictness in even the most common and undemanding of contexts, and in situations in particular to which angular accuracy would not seem to be essential. Nor can it be said that the word has a calculated geometric sense—like that of "straight," "right angle," or "triangle"—such that it must be used exactly or not at all. Actually, the use of "opposite" is, if anything, rather less rigorous in geometry than in ordinary speech; it is employed in an indicative or expository way, as in "the side opposite the right angle," not as a strict term of proof. So the punctilious use of the concept of opposition, in the spatial contexts of everyday description, is indeed all the more striking.

But, all the same, we have not yet glimpsed an answer to the question whether the recognition of opposition is an intellectual necessity. The nearest we have come to that point is in the inference that some special factor must be responsible for the exactitude of English usage. At first this accuracy in estimating opposition was ascribed to the compulsion of language, and of course this is the indispensable means by which the relation is impressed on the individual consciousness, but this fact does not explain the source of the compulsion. Furthermore, the evidence for this pressure comes from only one language. All that the comparative survey shows, on this score, is that the concept of opposition seems to be recognized in all languages, and it is from this that we infer that it is universally determined by some factor or factors independent of the nature of any particular language. Even if the ethnography of English usage is accepted as it has been sketched here, it does not follow that its constancy and precision in the employment of "opposite" will be replicated in other languages with regard to their equivalent words. As a matter of fact, there appears to be no readily discoverable information on these counts, and perhaps it is not yet likely that there should be. What would be required, in order to respond comparatively to the present question, are studies like Marshall Morris's pioneering ethnography of discourse in Puerto Rico (1981), only devoted especially to the topic of opposition. (Interestingly, Morris does give examples of the confusion of opposites [p. 44], but these pertain to phenomena that, so far, we are not in a position to treat.) In the absence of such studies, we are left with the inferences from lexical equivalents in their possible relation to the features of English usage. We may be inclined to see as plausible a propensity of thought toward opposition, but the evidences tending this way are not evidence that the concept is necessary.

The concept has not of course to be necessary in order to retain its general significance among modes of thought, or to claim a place among basic predicates, but if it is either universal or apparently unevadable we need to find out why. Perhaps we shall do better if we proceed to examine the concept of opposition in relation to other concepts with which it may be connected not semantically but formally.

Four

Formalism

Nothing is harder in philosophy
than to grasp an issue right from the beginning
and yet in treating it
to make use of knowledge that one has acquired.

G. C. Lichtenberg

I

The explication of Steinberg's drawing (above, chap. 2) was carried out by reference to dyadic contrasts. Such contrasts were subsumed under the general concept of opposition. This concept appears to be universally recognized in language as an indicator of relative location.

The spatial description "opposite" has, however, a metaphorical employment in reference to things that have no position in space; for example, good is said to be the opposite of evil. This spatial metaphor has long been given a prominent application in logic, and statements of opposition have been classified formally into various kinds. These kinds are distinguished by quantity, according as they refer to all or some, and by quality, according as the statements are affirmative or negative. There are in addition subsidiary distinctions and connections that are made, in other respects, among such opposites. Not all statements involve opposition, and not all terms are regarded as possessing opposites, but the metaphorical relation is assigned to logic, morality, symbolism, and an indeterminate range of significant statements and operations. The formal analysis of the employment of the spatial metaphor of opposition, in this very extensive semantic field, is a necessary part of the inquiry that we have undertaken.

The pioneer in the systematic analysis of opposites and opposite statements was Aristotle. There is no need, however, to go into his arguments in very great detail. There are convenient English translations of the *Categories* and *De Interpretatione* (trans. Ackrill 1963), and of the *Metaphysics* (trans. Warrington 1961). (These versions, with their pagination, will be cited below; classicists will easily find the corresponding places in the scholarly editions.) The entire topic, moreover, has been most compendiously treated by Geoffrey Lloyd in his *Polarity and Analogy* (1966). We need to start with a brief sketch of Aristotle's views, all the same, for two main reasons. The first is that his various remarks about opposites establish distinctions and criteria that any systematic examination of the subject has eventually to take into account, and his terminology still continues therefore to influence our own. The second reason is that we have to be familiar with Aristotle's typology in order to be in a position to transcend it, if only for the reason that we are acquainted with languages, social facts, and speculations that he did not know of, and we cannot presume that his ideas will accommodate these. So although it will be requisite to some extent to set out certain discrepancies, or else possibilities of variant interpretations, the point of the present survey will not be to determine the absolute sense of one or another term of analysis but to grasp his typology.

Aristotle, then, gives rather different lists of types of opposite at different places. In the *Categories,* he writes: "Things are said to be opposed to one another in four ways: as relatives or as contraries or as privation and possession or as affirmation and negation" (1963:31). In the later *Metaphysics,* he lists opposites, in Book *Δ,* as (1) contradictories, (2) contraries, (3) relative terms, (4) positive terms and their privatives, (5) the termini of generation and destruction, and (6) incompatible attributes (or their elements) of matter which is receptive of both (1961:20). In Book *I,* however, he writes that "the kinds of opposition are contradiction, privation, contrariety, and relation" (1961:314). Let us concentrate on the types that are common to the three lists (cf. Lloyd 1966:161). The first list cited provides a convenient order, as will be seen.

1. Relative (or correlative) terms are exemplified by "the double and the half"; things opposed as relatives are called "just what they are, *of* their opposites or in some other way *in relation* to one another" (1963:31, 32). Knowledge and the knowable are also so opposed; knowledge is of what can be known, and the knowable is such in relation to knowledge. We might add as examples of correlative opposition: senior/junior, predecessor/successor, mother/child. In each of these instances one term is (what it is) of the other or in relation to the other.

2. Contraries are by no means so straightforward. Unlike correlatives, they are not what they are *of* one another, though they are called contraries of one another; thus good is not called the good of the bad, but the contrary of it; and

so also with black/white. Aristotle at first distinguishes, in the *Categories,* two kinds of contraries, according to whether they do or do not admit an intermediate between the contrary terms. "If contraries are such that it is necessary for one or the other of them to belong to the things they naturally occur in or are predicated of, there is nothing intermediate between them" (1963:32). For instance, odd and even are predicated of numbers, and it is necessary for one or the other to belong to a number, either odd or even; between these there is certainly nothing intermediate. But if it is not necessary for the one or the other to belong to the thing, then there is something intermediate between them. For instance, black and white naturally occur in bodies, but it is not necessary for one or the other to belong to a body, for not every body is either white or black; between these hues are gray and yellow "and all other colours" (1963:33). So also with bad and good, for it is not necessary that any man or thing be either good or bad; between the good and the bad is the neither good nor bad. In some cases there exist names for the intermediates, as with gray and yellow; in other cases it is not easy to find a name for the intermediate, "but it is by the negation of each of the extremes that the intermediate is marked off, as with the neither good nor bad and neither just nor unjust" (1963:33).

In the *Metaphysics,* however, at Book Δ, Aristotle gives a more elaborate account of contraries. The adjective "contrary" is applied (1) to attributes differing in genus and incapable of belonging to the same subject at the same time; (2) to the most different attributes within the same genus or in the same subject matter, or falling within the sphere of one faculty; and (3) to things whose difference is greatest either absolutely or else with respect to genus or species.

Other things are called contrary in virtue of some relation (e.g., possession, receptiveness, action, passivity). Indeed, "'contrary' . . . must have a separate meaning corresponding to each category" (1961:20). In Book *I*, Aristotle writes that things may differ from one another in a greater or lesser degree, and that there is "a maximum difference" which he calls contrariety (1961:313); that which is maximum in each class is complete, so that contrariety is complete difference, "the meaning of complete varying with that of 'contrary'." As for intermediates, Aristotle devotes a separate argument to them (1963:320–21) in which he starts from the premise that "contraries admit of an intermediate, and in the majority of cases have one," and that intermediates must be composed out of contraries. In general, all intermediates lie between opposites of some kind; among opposites, contradictories admit of no mean, and relative terms which are not contrary have no intermediate. In sum, "all intermediates are (1) in the same genus, (2) between contraries, and (3) composed of these contraries." There are numerous further considerations, particularly in justification of these conclusions, but it is not necessary that we rehearse these before passing on to the next type of opposition.

3. Privation and possession, in the *Categories*, are said to be spoken of in connection with the same thing; for example, sight and blindness in connection with the eye. Each of them is spoken of in connection with whatever the possession naturally occurs in; what does not have sight cannot be called blind (1963:33). Privation and possession are plainly not opposed as relatives, nor are cases of privation and possession opposed as contraries. This latter assertion is argued in relation to contraries that have an intermediate, and also in relation to contraries that have no

intermediate (1963:34–35), but it is necessary to apprehend only this point, not the details of the proof.

4. Affirmation and negation stand quite apart from the preceding types of opposition. Aristotle stresses the difference when he writes, in the *Categories,* of things opposed as affirmation and negation that "only with them is it necessary always for one to be true and the other one false" (1963:36–37). For, he continues, with contraries it is not necessary always for one to be true and the other false, nor with relatives nor with possession and privation. "Nothing, in fact, that is said without combination is either true or false" (cf. Ackrill 1963:73–74; Lloyd 1966:161 n. 2). What this means is confirmed in *De Interpretatione,* where Aristotle writes: "Let us call an affirmation and a negation which are opposite a *contradiction*. I speak of statements as opposite when they affirm and deny the same thing of the same thing" (1963:47). Subsequently a distinction is drawn between contradictory opposites when what the one signifies universally the other signifies not universally (e.g., "every man is white"/"not every man is white") and contrary opposites in which a universal affirmation is opposed to a universal negation (e.g., "every man is just"/"no man is just"). The opposition of affirmation and negation is thus indeed different from the other types of opposition, in that it has to do with propositions that are capable of being true or false. This type of opposition, in other words, pertains to logic, whereas the others are defined in the *Categories* by reference to terms. Thus, to take a ready example, Aristotle could not have said (and in fact did not say) that "male" and "female" are contradictories.

It does not seem necessary, for our present purpose, to examine separately the two other types of opposition that Aristotle mentions, namely the termini of generation and destruction, and incompatible attributes of matter which is receptive of both. The former has a special connection with ontology, the latter has a problematic connection with contrariety. They may well be important for an understanding of every expression of Aristotle's thought about opposites, but our own concern is, rather, to determine what there is in his typology that we can rely on in our own thought about the kinds of conceptual phenomena that we have encountered under the heading of opposition.

II

Before we consider in what pragmatic respects Aristotle's typology may be reliable, there are some questions and qualifications that propose themselves.

It is difficult for a comparativist to deal confidently with these issues. On the one hand, there is no English commentary on the *Categories* and *De Interpretatione,* and no recent commentary in any language (Ackrill 1963 : v), and it is not the business of someone who is not a classical philosopher to attempt a critical exegesis. On the other hand, the philosophical literature on Aristotle, touching certainly on such matters as opposition, is vast, so there can be no definite claim that any of the present queries is either novel or unanswered. The point, nevertheless, remains that we are looking to Aristotle for initial direction in coming to terms with matters that philosophers are not normally concerned with, and there may be a distinct interest in such a venture. It should be kept in mind, also, that our overriding purpose is to test the claim of opposition to acceptance as a basic predicate, and this is a kind of problem that underlies any form of disciplined inquiry into social facts.

The first question, then, about Aristotle's typology is raised by its heterogeneity. Lloyd observes that one of the "striking features" of this classification of opposites is that oppositions between propositions (affirmations and negations) are dealt with alongside oppositions between terms (contraries, correlative opposites, and positive and privative terms) (Lloyd 1966:161–62). If it seems a little strange, he continues, that Aristotle should group contradictions alongside oppositions between terms, we see that this allows him to emphasize that "it is *only* in the case of contradictories that it is necessary that one of the pair must be true and the other false" (1966:163). Against the history of previous treatments of opposition by Greek philosophers, it can be held to Aristotle's credit that he revealed for the first time the precise conditions in which various opposites are to be judged as true or false; and then it is of great importance that he was also the first philosopher to carry out a full analysis of different types of opposite statements.

This is a distinct and admirable achievement in logic, but what has it to do with opposites that, being simply between terms, are not propositional? In other words, why call them all opposites? It cannot be said that all four types have it in common that they are dyadic, for as in Aristotle's later formulation in particular there are contraries that admit intermediates, so that the set of terms thus defined is actually triadic at least. The earlier argument, that certain contraries do not admit intermediates, made at any rate this assimilation to contradictories: that such contraries were dyadic and that there was nothing between them. But these facts alone would not self-evidently explain why the two types of dyadic relation should be grouped together, let alone why they should both be called opposites. And, after all, if it was a theoretical advance for Aristotle to demonstrate that only in contradictory (propositional) opposites was it necessary that one of the pair be true and the other false, then this differentia in itself provides a reason not to group contradictories with contraries and the rest. The point in classing things together is to say something about these things as members in common of that class, not to say that they are different.

A subsidiary question is why correlative terms should be called opposites. The examples mentioned do not explain the appellation. Double and half are the products of inverse arithmetical operations; knowledge, as what is known, and the knowable, or what can be known, are not connected in this way. So it is not plain why either should be called an opposition, or why the two examples should be classed together as instances of opposition. Similar considerations apply to senior/junior, predecessor/successor, and mother/child. It is apt and sufficient to call such pairs of terms correlatives, but why then go on to call them opposites as well? The effect of doing so is to class them with pairs (and propositions) to which they are dissimilar, and this is an outcome calling for a special justification that is not evident.

As for contraries, the position is even more difficult. There are sustainable arguments that they may or may not and always do admit intermediates; and there are in any event three kinds of contraries, and also additional ways in which things may be contrary in virtue of "some relation" to contraries, not to mention the "separate meaning [of 'contrariety'] corresponding to each category" (1961:20). Here, too, the definition of each kind is, or could be made, apt and sufficient by reference to its proper attributes, and it is a question why the kinds should not be distinguished by individual appellations instead of being classed together under a heading that subsumes a variety of dissimilarities. With particular regard to intermediates, moreover, Aristotle's use of words for these is found to be "rather loose" (Lloyd 1966:162), and, even after Lloyd's helpful clarification by reference to true or strict intermediates, there is a problem about their function in the typology. If it is entertained that all contraries do admit intermediates, this seems insufficient ground to class them together, since in one sense or another some correlatives and terms of possession and privation admit of intermediates too. So on the one hand there is a variety of intermediates, calling for individual specification, and on the other hand the dual variegation of intermediates and kinds of contraries has been grouped under the unitary term "contrary"—and then this grouping of disparate conceptual objects is unified under the name of "opposites." It could be suggested that this is not synthesis but conglomeration.

These queries and resistances do not necessarily attach to the uses that Aristotle makes of his typology of opposites in various methods of argument that he recommends or employs in the *Organon* or elsewhere (see Lloyd 1966:165). We are concerned here with the reliability of his distinctions in the analysis of representations other than his own examples, and especially representations that are not linked logically into an argument but instead compose a semantic scheme. In order to test that reliability, we shall consider by the present criteria the "opposites" that were isolated in the explication of Steinberg's drawing.

III

Let us first run through the phenomenal contrasts listed in table 2. It is at once evident that we can leave contradictory opposition (affirmation and negation) out of account, for none of the contrasts is propositional; that is, in neither column is anything affirmed or anything denied, and in no dyad are the terms opposed as true/false in respect of the same subject and the same predicate (see Lloyd 1966:163 n. 1). This leaves as possibly relevant distinctions the types of opposition relating to terms; there is hence a particular connection with the *Categories,* which "deals with terms, the constituents of propositions" (Ackrill 1963:69). The terms in table 2 are substantives, descriptive attributes, and certain spatial predicates.

The upper E and the lower E stand in a relationship that does not obviously qualify as an opposition. They are not, at any rate, correlatives or possessive/privative. They are separate instances of the same capital letter, differing (within the descriptions provided by these two terms alone) in that one is the upper and the other the lower. It could be said that, if we take the spatial qualifiers as proper attributes, the two letters are species within one genus (the letter). The differentiation does not, however, constitute a contrary: the terms do not fit any of Aristotle's three main types. The second type of contrary looks the most nearly accommodating, but the spatial predicates "upper" and "lower" are not the most different attributes within the same genus; they are relative attributes qualifying the respective locations of the two letters. These considerations do not, however, make it incorrect, by other criteria, to speak of the relationship between the two letters E as an opposition. The point presently at issue is that the Aristotelian typology does not serve, except conceivably by elimination, to define the respects in which the relationship should be described as an opposition.

The prospect improves, though, in the case of the second dyad: above/below. These are correlative terms, and together they constitute an opposition of that type; the idea of above entails that of below, and conversely. This instance poses nevertheless two problems. The first is that the dyad is not given in a direct descriptive sense, as are, for example, the three dimensions of the lower E. The relation is a consequence of the convention that the drawing has a right way up, and of the fact that in this setting one E is the upper and the other the lower. The abstraction corresponds, in this instance, to the locations of the two letters with respect to each other, but the correlative above/below is also an abstraction from these locations. Yet we have assumed above that the two letters as such are not correlatives. The second problem is connected with the first. Aristotle writes that what underlies an affirmation and a negation is not itself an affirmation or a negation, but that the underlying things "are said to be opposed to one another as affirmation and negation are" (1963:34). Even though this is a different mode of opposition, the question arises why as much should not be said of the things underlying a correlative such as above/below. If the two letters E underlie, or are the subjects of, the correlative opposition above/below, should not they also be regarded as correlatives after all? Something hangs on whether the phrase "are said to be" is taken idiomatically or analytically, but in either case the question stands. The pragmatic difficulty is not that this question, as also certain subsidiary questions, cannot be resolved, but that there should be such a question at all.

The dyad ethereal/terrestrial can be assigned to the first type of contrary opposition, namely that of attributes differing in genus and incapable of belonging to the same subject at the same time. There is, incidentally, nothing intermediate between them. The same can be said of the dyad two-dimensional/three-dimensional; these terms too are contraries with nothing intermediate (no other number of dimensions) to them. The dyad slender/squat, however, is not so easily treated, if only because the terms are not purely descriptive but can be read as reflecting esthetic values; by another assessment the upper E could be disparaged as attenuated, and the lower E praised as sturdy. If we take the terms as they stand, however, they can be opposed as contraries of the second type, namely, as attributes that are the most different within the same genus, or the same subject matter, or falling within the sphere of one faculty (1961:20). In this instance the opposition does admit intermediates, whether strict or defined by negation of each of the extremes; we can say that something between slender and squat is medium-shaped, or else that it is neither slender nor squat. So also with light/ponderous, which is a contrary of the second type, admitting intermediates. The next dyad, accented/plain, registers a diacritical difference by which it can be seen as a contrary of the first type; a letter capable of bearing an accent either has one or not, and there is no intermediate. Also of this type, and admitting no intermediate, is the dyad imaginary/concrete, terms that differ in genus.

The remaining constituents of the scheme, after the letters and their attributes, can be characterized fairly quickly. Cat and dog are contrary in the third type, by genus, with no intermediate. Chick and hen are contrasted by age and by size, the normal contrasts between infant and adult; they can be assigned to the second type of contrary, with at least an intermediate by negation of the extremes. Flower and weed differ in genus and constitute contraries of the third type, with no intermediate. The attributes cultivated/untended, qualifying flower and weed respectively, are opposed as contraries of the second type, with no intermediate. Finally, the potted bloom and the wild flower are "other in species" (1961:20), let us assume, and might be said to be opposed as contraries of the second type (the most different attributes within the same genus) if they were certainly contraries, but this is unsure. There is no intermediate between potted and unpotted; but there is an intermediate between a potted bloom and a wild flower, namely in the case of a flower tended in a garden bed.

IV

The assignment of dyads in the table to types of opposition in Aristotle's classification has not been entirely straightforward, and in certain instances some decisive effort or even forcing was called for.

These difficulties subsisted even though numerous other possibilities of complication were not taken into account; these would include the logic of division, the definition of a conceptual class, the notion of privation, and the criteria of an attribute "naturally occurring" in a thing. To a classical scholar, moreover, there will no doubt occur yet more uncertainties, as well perhaps as the alternative typing of one or another dyad. All of these factors combine to make it appear that Aristotle's typology of opposites is not the most advantageous for the present purpose.

The outcome, at any rate, can be summarized as in table 4. One dyad was unclassified, and one instance of type-two contrariety was unsure. Two types of contrary were unrepresented: type one with intermediate, and type three with intermediate. The positive results are that thirteen dyads are distributed among five kinds of opposition; and that,

TABLE 4
Aristotelian Opposites

correlatives	1
contraries type 1	5
contraries type 2	1
contraries type 2 + intermediates	4
contraries type 3	1
(unclassified)	1

among four types of contrary, one type (represented by three, or possibly four, dyads) admits intermediates. Table 3 could be subjected to a similar analysis, though with greater uncertainty since its terms are evaluative, not descriptive, and are either inferred or ascribed. We shall not demonstrate as much, but may proceed to consider the results of analyzing table 2 by Aristotelian criteria.

The main finding is that the table of opposites is not ordered by a single mode of opposition but by no fewer than five different modes (cf. Needham 1980:51–52). This might seem a useful conclusion, if it were not for certain reservations. In the first place, the proper attributes of each dyad, and their differences from one dyad to another, were already patent in the phenomenal description and in the explication of the scheme carried out in chapter 2. Indeed, it could well have appeared likely that more than five modes of opposition would be discriminable in the table. This introduces a second reservation. Other sets of criteria for the classification of opposites are feasible, and it is predictable that each set would assign the dyads to a different number of modes of opposition and to different groupings among themselves. What we need, however, is a reason to adopt one classification of opposites rather than another. The reason must depend on the purpose for which the analysis, by any criteria, is carried out.

Our present purpose in this chapter has been to examine the pragmatic cogency of the first and most famous systematic analysis of contrasted terms denoted by the spatial metaphor of opposition. That it was indeed a spatial metaphor is clear from early Greek usage. The key word is *antios*. Lloyd explains that this was already used by Homer, generally in a local sense, to mean "face to face," usually of persons such as opposing armies but sometimes of things such as two promontories facing each other across the entrance to a harbor. The word was first used in a cosmological context by Parmenides (sixth century B.C.), in reference to Light and Night; *enantios,* opposite, was used by medical writers in the context of the theory that opposites cure diseases caused by opposites; and the related *antixoos,* opposed to, adverse, occurred first in Heraclitus and thereafter was common in Ionic Greek (Lloyd 1966:126 n. 2). Aristotle used a variety of words for different kinds of opposites, but all were formed on *anti-* (p. 164 n. 3), connoting over against, opposite. (In this connection, incidentally, it is particularly important for the general reader that Ackrill should stress that in his translation "the word translated 'opposite' is always so translated" and that the corresponding noun is translated as "opposition." Ackrill 1963: 128.) For opposites generally, Aristotle uses *antikeimenon* and the like, connoting set over against, to correspond with, to be opposite to in respect of places and things.

It can readily be accepted, then, that in Aristotle's typology of opposites we really are dealing with a spatial relation, as in English and in other languages, that is extended metaphorically to relations between terms and between propositions. Yet whereas the denotation of the spatial relation is simple, and easy to exemplify (armies, promontories), the employment of the metaphor is complicated, and the examples of its use give rise to many reservations, qualifications, and problems. Defensible as each one of Aristotle's types may be, for his own logical purposes, it is not clear on what grounds the comparativist should accept that they are all species of the genus opposition. We have been trying, through Aristotle's thorough and ingenious writings on this topic, to test the claim to acceptance of the concept of opposition as a basic predicate. But what we discover instead is that corresponding to our spatial metaphor there is in the Greek of the fourth century B.C. an equally metaphorical elaboration of the idea. The examination conducted so far has given no satisfactory reason to prefer that metaphor to our own, or to think that "opposition" denotes a unitary mode of relation the true character of which has been revealed by formal analysis.

It might be objected that the pragmatic test we have carried out, by reference to Steinberg's drawing, is not appropriate because of the nature of the materials. The drawing is, after all, the product of a highly idiosyncratic imagination, so if Aristotle's types do not fit its scheme effectively there is nothing to be wondered at. Well, in the first place we have not yet determined what it would mean for an analysis of oppositions to be rated as appropriate or effective. Certainly it cannot be presumed that the outcome shall be the discernment of a single articulating mode of relation among a set of any oppositions whatever. Secondly, it has not yet appeared that Steinberg's scheme, for all its singularity as a graphic invention, is in any systematic respect untypical. Even if it were unusual in some respects, it would still be an expression, to the extent that it is an oppositional scheme, of a factor that has been presumed to be basic and thus operative in any human consciousness. Finally, even though the drawing is singular, the objects and values out of which it is composed are entirely familiar and, to western eyes, culturally significant. If opposition has the fundamental importance claimed for it, and if it can be discerned in Steinberg's drawing, a theory of opposites such as that of Aristotle should be applicable to the drawing, and as effectively as to any other scheme of opposites, but it is not.

Five

Lexicology

But if it be a question of words and names,
. . . look ye to it.

Acts 18:15

I

Two and a quarter millennia after the death of Aristotle, the time was thought right for a "fresh start" in the analysis of opposition. This was the determination of C. K. Ogden, author of *Opposition* (first published in 1932), a work that was to be described by I. A. Richards (in Ogden 1967:8) as an "extraordinary piece of original and seminal lexicological experimentation."

Ogden referred to Aristotle as having been obsessed by the problem of opposition (1967:21), but he viewed Aristotle's work as resting on a "naive verbal basis" (p. 23). "His complete dependence on one language . . . was hardly less of a handicap than the primitive state of Greek science" (p. 24). In principle, and especially from the point of view of comparativism, these may appear plausible imputations, but they do not strike as squarely as the words are direct. Aristotle's distinctions among opposites, expressed in Greek of the fourth century B.C., were translated into Arabic and Latin, and thereafter into numerous languages of Europe and elsewhere, yet scholars could readily accord on the sense of what he had written; and when they dissented from his analyses it has not prominently been charged against him that he was misled or handicapped by his dependence on the Greek language alone. Benveniste has indeed demonstrated that Aristotle's decalogue of categories reflects "the structure of classes of a particular language" rather than absolute necessities of thought (1966, chap. 6), but this criticism does not attach directly to the analysis of opposition. Moreover, it is not commonly held that dissent among exegetes over points of interpretation of Aristotle's arguments has been occasioned by differences among their own languages. In chapter 4, certainly, we have encountered no hint that there are linguistic impediments in the way of grasping Aristotle's criteria for the discrimination of types of opposites. There were numerous queries and problems about his typology, but these were premised on the tacit conviction that it was perfectly possible to understand what he meant. The reliance on translations made into twentieth-century English was founded, also, on the explicit stipulation that each of Aristotle's lexical distinctions was translatable into a corresponding distinction in English. This correspondence was not the product of a convenient (or equally hampering) similarity of idiom between two Indo-European languages: it was produced by means of a formal analysis that is as apt in English as it is in classical Greek.

Paradoxically, Ogden's own analysis of opposition is in its turn completely dependent on one language, and its chief strength is actually that it concentrates so ingeniously on the idiom of opposition in English. Although Ogden begins by asserting that "an analysis of the nature of opposition" is fundamental for all work on a universal language (1967: 17), it emerges that his real interest is in Basic English (pp. 105–8; see also 56, 92). Yet, as will be seen, the advantage promised by Ogden's work is that the criteria of his analysis are quasi-geometrical, not grammatical, so that they ought to be applicable to any natural language.

II

The material for Ogden's analysis consists of twenty-five pairs of words "said to have opposites in the ordinary sense of this term" (see table 5). They are reported to have been taken at random, which would have been hard enough to do; but at the same time their sources are given as "works on lexicology, psychology, and logic" (p. 53), which must mean that in effect they are quite specially selected. The pairs are nouns and adjectives in English, and the point of view from which they are examined is that of members of the English linguistic tradition. These too, however, are rather select. Ogden says that if his list were presented to "a dozen persons of intelligence and experience" (p. 54), with no special training in psychology or traditional logic, it is probable that all the pairs would be passed as "opposites" by one or another of this group, while twenty of the twenty-five pairs would be likely to secure a majority vote. Ogden's premises and sampling procedures may not be all that satisfactory, but let us admit that the pairs in his list could

TABLE 5
Ogden's Opposites

black	white
hot	cold
open	shut
ruler	ruled
hard	soft
right	left
man	brute
up	down
acid	alkali
pleasure	pain
visible	invisible
town	country
learned	ignorant
possible	impossible
kind	unkind
good	bad
work	play
ill	well [*sic*]
easy	difficult
before	after
male	female
love	hate
British	alien
red	green
normal	abnormal

in one sense or another—whether or not "the ordinary sense"—be seen as opposites. The important thing, after all, is what he makes of them, and it is here that he comes into his own.

He begins by remarking that three pairs (man/brute, town/country, male/female) raise questions of a verbal nature involving the theory of definition. That of red/green is to some the most fundamental opposition in the list, but by others is the most summarily rejected. Also, "at all points the nature of Negation proves hardly less puzzling to the practical mind than the vagaries of linguistic usage" (p. 54). Why, he asks, is "not-white" so unsatisfactory to deal with, while "not-visible" or "invisible" readily recommends itself as the opposite of "visible"? The writings of logicians, he finds, are intriguing rather than helpful, and we are left with "a general impression of vagueness" (p. 56). So the task remains to see what more can be done about the "five-and-twenty candidates" in the list.

In the first place, Ogden continues, on the purely verbal level "it is curious that some words seem to have such obvious and universal opposites, while others seem to resist all attempts to contrast them in this way with incompatible partners" (p. 56). Or, again, whereas the repugnance of red and blue is not counted as an opposition, what about black and white (p. 57)? It is the study of the visual field and of contrasts between colors that then leads to Ogden's fundamental distinction (pp. 58–59):

Opposition . . . may be either the two extremes of a scale or the two sides of a cut; the cut marking the point of neutrality, the absence of either of two opposed characters in the field of opposition. By a cut, moreover, we can dichotomize either a "linear projection" or a "field of referents."

Spatial opposites generated by a cut are thus different in many respects from series opposites. "If we decide that Inside and Outside are opposites generated by a cut, there is no question of a series, and the one side is finite while the other is infinite" (p. 59). Although Ogden concedes that we can speak of "further inside" and can distinguish degrees of exteriority, thus making a quantitative gradation on either side of the dividing line, "this is a secondary consideration, and it is significant that the opposition begins, as it were, immediately the line is crossed."

III

With this initial example we are at once in possession of a principle, and we are also implicated in critical uncertainties.

Ogden begins from the premise that we "decide" that inside/outside are opposites generated by a cut. (This opposition, it will be noted as a curiosity, is not one of the twenty-five pairs in the list.) If there is "no question" of a series, this is no more than a consequence by definition: the consequence does not confirm the decision, and the grounds for deciding so have not been stipulated. When Ogden states that degrees of inside or outside are secondary, this is in part a consequence of the decision that the opposition is generated by a cut, and in part it is an arbitrary and rhetorical contrast of definitive value between components of one and the same situation. Let us therefore take another look at this situation.

Logically, of course, inside and outside are mutually exclusive: something that, from a given point of observation, is inside with respect to a certain limit cannot simultaneously be outside with respect to that same limit. But this does not entail that inside/outside is an instance of opposition (if that is what it is) by cut and not by scale: if it did, there would be no need for us to "decide" that it is generated by a cut. The distinction at issue is not logical but is part of our everyday descriptive vocabulary, and this fact is no doubt a reason that we have to make a decision in the present instance. Inside and outside are not normally taken in isolation; their operative value comes into play in statements, and these statements have to do with situations that may well lack the factitious clarity of logic. For example, when someone is charged under English common law with breaking and entering, it has to be determined whether or not he was inside the property in question. There are numerous cases demonstrating that this is in fact an imprecise and contentious matter, and sometimes such as has to be settled by a judgment of the court. The uncertainty is not the result of ignorance of where precisely the boundary to the property is; this may be absolutely sure, and yet there can be doubt as to whether or not the defendant was inside it. So in such a case the conceptual clarity of inside/outside is not replicated in the assessment of an action.

Moreover, Ogden goes on to consider rectangles, buildings, streets, and rivers as instances of "a peculiar kind of opposition," and he concludes that "for practical purposes we can regard our Cut itself as varying in breadth" (p. 60). Indeed, the cut can be, rather surprisingly, "rectilinear or circular, wide or purely linear," and it admits "various possibilities of gradation" (p. 66). If this is so (and it is a matter for Ogden himself to decide), we have, formally speaking, a triad: opposite a–an extent–opposite b. The terms a and b may be said to be opposed, but the opposition does not begin, as Ogden says it does, immediately a line is crossed. Instead of a dyad, we have in the components of this situation a sequence which might indeed seem to qualify as a series, so that in such a case we are dealing not with a cut but with a scale, for there must be gradations through the "breadth" between a and b. This matter of gradation, which might have been thought inconsistent with the concept of a cut, can be illustrated by considerations that Ogden says are secondary. In fact, each of his characterizations of inside/outside, in relation to "quantitative gradation" (p. 59), is disputable.

First, he says that "the one side is finite while the other is infinite"; evidently, inside is taken to be finite and outside infinite, as in his diagram (p. 16). This could be so from the point of view of someone inside a bounded space such as an automobile or a cell or a house, but there are other relevant situations. Consider a forest and a plain. In reality the trees could become sparser in the direction of the plain, so that there would be some extent which was neither true forest nor true plain. But let us assume, in Ogden's favor, a simpler case: there is a definite boundary, on the plain-side of which there is not a single tree. This replicates the pictorial clarity of the cut, but the alleged contrast need not obtain. There is no reason to assume that the forest is any more finite than is the plain, and someone who enters the forest from the plain can go deeper and deeper inside it. It is not even clear, either, that the opposition inside/outside begins immediately the line (the boundary that we have supposed) is crossed. This is a matter of idiom, and in ordinary English discourse what we have here is an approximation to a series or indeed a scale.

Let us consider again the case of someone coming from the plain and entering the forest. He can be first far outside the forest, then right outside, and afterwards just outside; on entering, he is first just inside, then right inside, and afterwards deep inside. This looks like a scale between the two extremes of plain and forest. Admitted, there is still a boundary that is crossed; our traveler is first on one side of it, then on the other. (There must be a point or extent at which he is on neither one side nor the other, though we do not ordinarily register this fact in our idiom of traversing a boundary.) Yet even this line tends to be blurred by our usual descriptions: "just outside" is practically speaking equivalent, as a description of location, to "almost inside," and "just inside" is comparably equivalent to "almost outside." Finally, by this account, such recognition of the line as survives no longer makes the appearance of a dichotomous cut between two unitary opposites. Instead, the line is a point, more or less precisely determined, midway on a scale running through a "field of referents." If it should be pressed that there is still that much of a line, all the same, the response would be that the range of discriminations within which it is found is very different from the simple cut between two opposite terms with which we began.

There is in fact a quite different view that can be taken of inside/outside. The cut, lying between two contrary extents of gradation (as marked by common idiom), is equivalent to the zero point on a centigrade thermometer. In the latter case the scale goes above zero in one direction, and below zero in the other direction. In these respects there can be said to be two scales end to end; one positive, the other negative. Nevertheless, there is a continuous scale of degrees of temperature running from one end of the mercury tube to the other. This is a paradigm of Ogden's scalar type of opposition, and yet it is closely matched by the range of discriminations subsumed under inside/outside, which Ogden presents as his opening example of opposition by cut.

The best that can be said of this example is that it shows that there is at least one opposition (perhaps: type of opposition) that can be analyzed in two ways: logically by cut, or idiomatically by scale. A more damaging conclusion is that Ogden's "very fundamental distinction in any theory of opposites" (p. 58), namely that between the cut and the scale, is framed by concepts that are not mutually exclusive. To judge by the critique of this one example, therefore, the methodological distinction is either ambiguous or confused. The example itself, however, may not be typical, despite the advanced position it occupies in Ogden's exposition; and perhaps the distinction can be proved fundamental, after all, in the analysis of other oppositions in the list (table 5).

IV

Before we look at that possibility there is a third feature in Ogden's model that needs to be reported. He thinks that the opposite sides of a cut and the opposite ends of a scale "will go a long way towards covering the cases of opposition with which lexicology is confronted" (p. 60), but that neither feature, as such, will help with opposite directions. The cases of two trains passing each other and of up/down, backwards/forwards, into/out of introduce a "new feature, *reversibility*" (p. 61).

The first comparison Ogden makes in this connection is between these "directional opposites" and that kind of opposition which is the product of "the same shape reversed." His concern here is to ask whether all of these opposites can be grouped under a single head. Mirror images, enantiomorphs, and all forms of geometrical reversal may be regarded as "directional opposites in rotation." There are no degrees between these opposites, as there are between the extremities of a scale, and there does not seem to be any very obvious relation to the principle of the cut. Ogden's very reasonable aim, then, is to find a way of unifying the different cases of opposition. As a preliminary to any attempt to discover "a common principle," he notes that "all motion at the heuristic level is either translational (rectilinear) or rotational" (p. 61). The pertinence of this premise is that the scale can be regarded as a diagram of rectilinear motion; psychological oppositions, "which are felt and described as pulling in opposite directions" (p. 62), can be diagrammed as rectilinear motion in opposite directions starting from a neutral point, the cut; and rotation, the other kind of directional opposition, completes the catalogue. The common principle of opposition, therefore, appears to be reversible direction. Indeed, Ogden later asserts that "in all opposition we are ultimately describing directions" (p. 92), and that "opposition is based on spatial experience"; "we are dealing with a visual schematism" (p. 94).

From this point, Ogden presses his analysis to its final stage, just as he attempts to disclose the ultimate grounds of opposition. "The symbolic forms which have been developed in ordinary language for the expression of these distinctions have been crystallized," he proposes, "not only in terms of two-dimensional projection, but also in a very special relation to the human body" (pp. 94–95). First, the spatial cut has been "identified with the body itself," and more especially with its vertical axis, in the opposition of the sides, right and left. Secondly, the extremes of the scale are "represented by the head and feet," the two opposite ends of a single continuum. Thirdly, the *op*- in Latin and the *gegen* in German "go back to" the asymmetry of the human body; "that which it faces, that which is placed over against (anti-contra-ob) it, is the primary opposite from which the long line of metaphor is derived" (pp. 96–97).

The essentials of this argument can be stated quite succinctly: the principle of opposition is reversible direction;

and (directional) opposites are based on the spatial experience of the human body.

It is an engaging feature of Ogden's style that he states a case by way of rapid assertions, not always pausing to demonstrate connections of evidence or argument between the points he wishes to make. I. A. Richards even alludes to "an almost cryptic verbal economy in his statements of most importance" (in Ogden 1967:9). It is possible with some sympathy to follow what he thinks, but not always the reasons for which he thinks as he does. In the present matter these deficiencies leave his contentions, fundamental though they are, open to criticism but on counts that perhaps he could have met in a more consequential method of argument. As the argument stands, however, it does not carry much conviction.

Ogden alludes very aptly to visual schematism, for this appears to be the characteristic way in which he himself formulates his ideas. Certainly the scale and the cut are spatial images, and their explication gives them a quasi-material form. In Ogden's diagram of opposites (p. 16) they have in fact definite material representations, and it is a likely inference that he thought out his problems in terms of these diagrammatic forms. This supposition would help us to understand how it is that he should write about conceptual opposites, having no location in space, as though they could be plotted by spatial coordinates. "In all opposition," he asserts, "we are ultimately describing directions" (p. 92); and the directions, whether implicating cut, scale, or reversibility, are conceived of in terms of "rectilinear motion" (pp. 60–63).

A persuasive way to interpret Ogden's mode of analysis is to suggest that an inclination to reificatory thought met a representation of like nature in the spatial idiom of opposition; one style of metaphor responded to the other, with the result that the analysis was subverted by its very subject matter. That it was subverted is shown by the inefficacy of the analytical apparatus when applied to certain instances of opposition.

One candidate is that of psychological oppositions, which allegedly are "felt and described as pulling in opposite directions" (p. 62). There is indeed a common phrase about being pulled or tugged in opposite directions by conflicting emotions or values; but it is most contestable that people actually "feel" themselves as pulled rather than as pushed or impelled or driven, and it is hard to imagine how they could sense the precise directions between which they were torn. What they can do, however, is to convey the intensity of their irresolution by means of the familiar phrase—and this form of words is yet another expression of the spatial metaphor of opposition. Here again the metaphor has taken over, and the constituents of its spatial idiom have been ascribed to the consciousness of individuals. That this is analytically mistaken, to say no more, is borne out by what Ogden does when he comes to the analysis of the psychological opposition of love and hate (p. 87). The instance is surely typical enough, yet in his analysis of it there is nothing at all about directions or rectilinear motion. Instead, Ogden refers to "intricate problems of definition," alludes to a list of comparable emotions, and concludes merely that "there will be a variety of cuts, with an even greater variety of linguistic anomalies in the total series."

Another example of the kind is Ogden's treatment of the opposition ruler/ruled (pp. 68–71). He identifies these emphatically as relative terms, and he proceeds to make a number of observations about correlatives, with particular reference to Aristotle; he makes some acute comparisons with eater/eaten, painter/painting, and so on, with special attention to the peculiarities of father/mother. But nowhere in this longish treatment does he introduce, let alone apply, the notions of reversible direction or rectilinear motion, any more than he resorts for an ultimate explanation to the human body.

V

Even where Ogden does make explicit use of his analytical distinctions, there must be considerable doubt that the method explains anything.

The first instance of opposition in his list is black/white, which he says gives a clear example of "the continuous scale," whether formed by least discriminable differences of light or pigment, or by gradual increments of light or pigment physically measured (p. 66). Alternatively, he adds, it might also be described as the scale of gray, with black and white as its limiting members. Either way, it is curious to represent black/white by a scale, as though this were the paradigmatic form of the opposition. The case might well be advanced that when these light-values are considered together as an opposition there is no assumption of any intermediates such as would compose a scale. Empirically, this is a matter for inquiry, but in principle it is at least a hypothetical construction that Ogden might well have taken into account. That he does not do so is perhaps to be explained by his reificatory inclination and by his consequent commitment to his diagrams of cut and scale. We have only to recall certain contexts in which black and white are contrasted as opposites in order to see how far that approach misses the point.

74

Black is commonly used to characterize moral attributes and inner states, not just pigmented surfaces or the absence of light. We can say that someone is black-hearted or is in a black state of mind; a deed can be black, and so can humor. White is the color of virtue, especially purity, and innocence. These are what we vaguely call symbolic uses of the color terms, and between them there are, in such instances, no intermediates, not other colors and not gradations of gray; in other words, there is no scale. Ethnography provides more striking proofs; for example, the impressive range of contrasted values, cosmological features, and modes of behavior which for the Nyoro are traditionally separated out by reference to black and to white (Needham 1973:310–12). Sometimes there is a symbolic intermediate between black and white, in particular red (Jacobson-Widding 1979; Needham 1981:38–40), but this third hue has its own distinct significance; it does not constitute, and does not imply, a scale of any kind. Typically, also, as in the Nyoro case, there are no direct connotations of a spatial significance in the moral confrontation of black with white, so that, in this respect as well, Ogden's paradigm finds no purchase.

Similar considerations apply to the opposition hard/ soft. Ogden treats these adjectives as pertaining to "a single scale of resistance to pressure," whereas plasticity gives another scale. "Sometimes, therefore, we are concerned with stretches on either side of a cut, sometimes with a scale and two extremes" (pp. 71–72). But these alternatives do not concede enough to the actual use of the words. Men may be characterized as hard in opposition to women, who are conceived of as soft; or a woman may be regarded as hard by contrast with the soft virtues imputed to her sex; one person has a hard life, another a soft life; hard words are disparaged in contrast with the soft answer that turneth away wrath. These are not scalar expressions, though they can be made such; a man may be hard (that is, hard-hearted), but not as hard as someone else. Even in this instance, though, it is not implied that there is a scale from an extreme hardness to an extreme softness. If there can be thought to be a cut, on the other hand, in that no third term is ordinarily interposed between hard and soft, taken as moral assessments, still there is no connection here with the direction and extent of spatial values.

When Ogden does come to an opposition that is "based on the structure and orientation of the human body" (p. 72), he has nothing very revealing to say about it. This is the opposition right/left, which he says gives us "a pair of directional opposites of a very fundamental kind." This is well enough, but the analytical apparatus provides no more than the comment that right and left are "exhaustive opposites based on an absolute cut." The subsequent observation, that enantiomorphs and the like are "explained" in terms of "rotational motion in opposite directions (right or left)," either claims too much in the way of explanation or else is no more than true by definition.

In other cases, Ogden frequently has interesting or provocative things to say, for example about the opposite of a circle, or on a screwdriver as the opposite of a screwdriver (p. 73), and he is helpful in pointing out that sometimes a variety of opposites may present themselves and that a name may or may not exist to fixate an opposition (p. 74), but it would not be profitable for us to work through all the other oppositions in his list. The main reason not to do so is that the analytical apparatus itself can already be seen not to be convincing; and certainly it is hard to agree that "in every case the directional factor is relevant" (p. 90). In some cases this factor is neither mentioned nor pertinent, for instance in the opposition male/female (pp. 86–87); and when it is in fact introduced it is typically, as we have observed, a diagrammatic or dynamic construction corresponding to the spatial metaphor of opposition.

VI

A concluding part of Ogden's monograph that should be mentioned in his form of notation, which is intended to "simplify the description of the various kinds of opposition" (p. 99).

This notation consists of a set of simple signs such as O, +, and −, with which are combined lower-case letters such as m, i, and d to indicate modes or aspects of the relation. Thus the opposition love/hate (see sec. IV above) is represented by: Love O + i + d Hate (p. 103). This is to be read as: Love is an opposite by cut scaled down to the cut, the side of the cut being named by its extreme point (namely love); the cut is scaled to indifference (i); the other side of the cut is scaled to an opposite by the negation of a definition (d) to the extreme point of hate. Ruler/ruled is represented by: Ruler O cor O d Ruled (p. 101) = ruler is opposed as correlative (though "only by special definition"), in opposition, by the negation of a definition, to ruled. Black/white is represented by: Black O−−White = black is an opposite in a continuous scale whose other extreme is its opposite, white. Hard/soft is represented by: Hard O + m + Soft = hard is an opposite by cut scaled down to the cut, this being registered by a medium (m) value, from which there is a scale down to soft. As the last of our examples, right/left is represented by: Right O O Left = right is the rectilinear directional opposite by cut of left.

By means of this notation the twenty-five examples of opposition are distributed among thirteen formal types. Ogden does not draw out this result, since his concern is to demonstrate the employment of his notation in the service of convenience, but it raises some questions. No fewer than four of the types include d, denoting an opposite by the negation of a definition; thus the simplest, Od, is the formula for town/country, work/play, ill/well, and male/female. Yet the analyses of these oppositions individually, though registering some points of similarity, do not establish that they are instances of one distinct kind of comparative estimation; and when the connotations of the terms are taken into account, the outcome is that by their respective definitions the oppositions are significantly different from one another. This much could be demonstrated in detail, but since the formulas sum up the analyses of the cases, and since the analyses are in principle or in practice not cogent, there would be no point in dragging out the argument so. (These are the main reasons, also, that no attempt will be made here to assort the oppositions of table 2 or table 3 according to Ogden's method or his notation.) Similar criticisms attach to the remaining formulas and their examples, with the result that the twenty-five cases could be seen as expressing twenty-five modes of opposition. Of course, similarities and differences are not simply given, so by one set of criteria or another the cases could certainly be classified in various ways. But the mere possibility of classifying opposites is not the issue. What calls for justification is Ogden's particular method of doing so. His criteria, as put to use in his analyses of individual cases, have been found disputable, and so therefore must be the formulas on the basis of which the opposites have in effect been classified.

What Ogden's treatment does very usefully achieve, however, is to show that there is no one mode of relation common to all of his examples and which is the basic form of opposition. There is indeed a common term to his thirteen types of formula, but this is simply the O, which means no more than that the words in each of the cases are defined as composing an opposition. When this sign is cancelled out as being analytically insignificant, each of the formulas is distinct from the others. Moreover, it should be possible to find examples of yet other formulas that could be composed with the signs of the notation. And then there are the differences of connotation, amounting to different modes, which further distinguish the examples grouped under one type. So in the end we are left to ask what it is that the types are types of. If it is "opposition," then there are at least that many types of this relation, and there are in addition many more numerous modes.

Yet what really has to be justified is Ogden's working premise that the cases in his list are all oppositions. Well, it can still be said, that is what they are. That is, they are regarded as oppositions, or they are likely to be identified as such, by speakers (or at any rate certain speakers) of the English language. They represent accepted or defensible uses of the word "opposite," and this various usage is what Ogden has succeeded in displaying. What he has not done is to prove that the concept of opposition is fundamental in any respect, let alone that it is a universal propensity or a logical necessity.

Six

Complementarity

When there is an obscurity too deepe for our reason,
'tis good to sit downe with a
description, periphrasis, or adumbration.

Sir Thomas Browne

I

At this point we can register some decided convergences
between the analyses carried out by our two exemplars.
Aristotle distinguishes formally among various modes of
opposition; his method rests on the logic of division (the
principles of hierarchical classification) and the logic of
propositions in Greek. Ogden distinguishes a different variety; his method is to seek diagrammatic distinctions among
expressions of opposition in English. The common outcome, from our point of view, is that there is no simple or
essential form to the postulated relation of opposition.

The variegation of modes of opposition has since been

clearly summed up by Lloyd (though he does not cite
Ogden's investigation) in a long chapter entitled precisely
"The Analysis of Different Modes of Opposition" (1966:
86–171). He begins indeed by stating that "the English
terms 'opposite' and 'opposition,' like the Greek *antikeíme-
non* and *antikeîsthai,* are used to refer to many different
types of relationship" (p. 86). He illustrates this assertion
by reference to Aristotle's distinctions, but he has also taken
into account "the comprehensive dualist classifications of
phenomena which anthropologists have reported from
various present-day societies" (p. 88; see also pp. 31–41).
His subsequent survey, which is unremittingly instructive
and well brings out the different concepts of opposition in
early Greek thought, extends from the Eleatic philosophers (fifth century B.C.) to Aristotle. The history is conclusive as to its main contention, culminating with the
demonstration that it was Aristotle who was the first philosopher to undertake a full analysis of the different modes
of opposition (p. 169). Lloyd's subject matter, however, is
argumentation and explanation, and, in the main, he does
not make it his concern to analyze opposition in yet deeper
and more comparative respects. His field of study, after all,
is the development of informal logic, and his evidence is
nothing less than the sum of Greek literature from Homer
to Aristotle (p. 9); it is not at all incumbent upon him to go
far beyond his already wide limits of scholarly commitment. All the same, it remains the case that, literally, he
takes the concept of opposition as given, so that what he
delineates are modes "of" opposition, as though this were
nonetheless essentially an autonomous relation or at least a
set of modes having a common focus. His argument examines the theories of Greek thinkers concerning topics that

are translatable as "opposition," and for the most part he does not address the underlying problem of whether opposition possesses intrinsic and distinctive features, so that he makes only passing allusions (which we shall examine later) to the occasions or the grounds of the type of relation.

A significant contrast is to be seen in two of Lloyd's concluding remarks at the end of his book. First he reiterates that Aristotle brought to light the "complexity" of the relationships of similarity and opposition (p. 435). Then he writes that, judged as "abstract schemata," the two main types of theories found to be particularly common in early Greek speculative thought—namely those based on polarity and analogy—both have obvious merits in terms of "their intelligibility, their simplicity and (in the case of those based on opposites, particularly) their apparent comprehensiveness" (pp. 437–38). It is this paradoxical combination of complexity with schematic concision that sets the scene for a resumed investigation into the many different types of relationship which are treated nevertheless as though they composed a single mode of relation. We are faced here, in the words of Sir Thomas Browne (1646, bk. 6, chap. 1), with an "authentick obscurity."

II

If we start again from a simple formula, we can represent opposition by an arrangement of signs such as: a/b. What in this little formula is given, and what must we read into it so that it shall qualify as a proper expression of the relation?

What is given, by a quasi-universal convention of written language, is that there are two terms, here represented by *a* and *b*. This dyadic base is the premise to Aristotle's formalism and to Ogden's list of examples, and it is also a principle by which the explication of Steinberg's drawing was carried out. For the moment, at any rate, what the terms of the formula stand for is indifferent: they could be epithets such as black and white, material objects such as two promontories, individuals such as king and subject, groups such as two armies, and so on. So far, also, there is no reason to exclude propositions, even though we know that logically they occupy a peculiar position, and that opposed propositions have attributes that are not to be found in the opposition of terms (which neither affirm nor deny). By long convention, contradictory propositions are said to be opposites, and there are in any instance two of them corresponding to *a* and *b*. But the fact that notionally there are only two terms in any instance of opposition (no matter that each term can stand for a plurality of things) does not provide a sufficient condition of the relationship.

Pairs of terms can be related by adjunction, conjunction, subsumption, alternation, mutual exclusion, and in other ways. So whereas it is necessary by definition that the relation of opposition shall hold between only two terms, this condition supplies merely the form of the relation. What remains crucially to be specified is the relationship, represented in our formula by the solidus (/), between the two terms *a* and *b*. That is, we are looking for a single hypothetical mode of relation that would justify the singular appellation of "opposition." Naturally, we could say that the solidus stands for whatever it happens to represent, in any instance, from among a variety of contrasts that are called oppositions; but this would merely replicate, by implication, the evidential complexity that has seemed to call instead for abstract analysis.

III

Within a given cultural tradition there is a significant link, which may be more or less clearly recognized, between things that are regarded as opposites one to the other. That is, they do not stand to each other simply (if at all) in a formal relationship that holds between other pairs of opposites as well, but there is a connection such that it is regarded as appropriate that the one should be opposed to the other.

This does not mean that for any particular thing (term, quality, or whatever) there is only one other such thing to which it can be opposed, but that within each such relationship it will be seen as proper that the thing shall be opposed to each other thing to which it is opposed. It would seem likely that there is in each instance of opposition, within the given tradition, a quality or condition that is the ground of the particular appropriateness. This kind of link may seem obvious in the case of correlatives such as right/left or above/below, and it would seem strange if the oppositions were instead right/below or left/above. But it is less obvious in the case of sun/moon, and not at all so with such Kaguru oppositions as red/white or sperm/blood (Beidelman 1973:151).

These latter cases are adduced as illustrations of the general feature of a significant link between opposites that are taken to belong together. It would be distracting to investigate, at this stage in the exposition, the particular qualities and conditions that mark particular cultural oppositions: the point to be taken is the premise that there is a general feature of appropriateness. Nevertheless, there are two methodological observations to be made in passing. One is that with such examples as those taken from Kaguru culture we are in the realm of what we shall just call, without any further stipulation, the symbolic. The second observation is connected with the first, namely that, since symbolism is characteristically not propositional, we shall not expect to have to deal with contradictions or, more generally, with logical opposition. These remarks are introduced here, not as matters to be accepted without demonstration, but in order to provide a sense of direction in the development of the argument. With this much of a parenthesis we can turn back to the main topic just introduced.

Let us take it, then, that opposites are appropriate to each other; in other words, that in an opposition the terms belong together. The secondary premise, that the significant link may be qualitatively distinct in each instance, can be set aside for the time being. Not that it is unimportant, but it concerns the particular instances of what has been posited as a general feature, and it is this feature that calls for initial attention. In order to provide that, it may be helpful to distinguish the feature by a special designation. In another context than that of a monograph on opposition, we might well say that opposites that are appropriate to each other, or that belong together, stand in a relation of apposition. Alternatively, we could say that they accord with each other or stand in accordance each with the other; but these phrases tend to eliminate the essential contrast between opposed terms, and by their connotations they also imply a propositional content. Let us therefore adopt a term from traditional logic and speak of the "connexity" of opposites.

This connexity, to resume, is a general feature of opposition, and it calls for an analysis that can eventually be formulated in abstract terms. Our empirical task, however, is to discern the grounds of connexity within the scope of comparative ethnography, and there is in fact a notion employed by social anthropologists that seems likely to provide an explanation of connexity in the special sense given to the term here. For a convenient source we may refer to a collective volume on dual symbolic classification published under the title *Right & Left* (Needham, ed. 1973). Throughout this work, beginning with the foreword by Evans-Pritchard (p. x) and in the essays by six of the contributors (Needham, Beidelman, Faron, Cunningham, Rigby, Middleton), there recurs the use of the words "complementary opposites" (see the index, s.v. Complementarity). The possibility thus suggests itself that the key to connexity may be complementarity.

The history of the use of the adjective "complementary" in anthropology is unclear, and in a nontechnical sense it may well have been employed sporadically for some time. One notable place, however, if not yet in specific connection with opposites, is Bateson's *Naven* (first ed. 1936), where it plays a part in the analysis of values in Iatmul society: "A relationship between two individuals (or between two groups) is said to be chiefly complementary if most of the behaviour of the one individual is culturally regarded as of one sort (e.g., assertive) while most of the behaviour of the other, when he replies, is culturally regarded as of a sort complementary to this (e.g., submissive)" (Bateson 1958:308 s.v.). This is illustrative rather than definitive, just as is the use of the word in the body of the text (pp. 176–77), and apparently Bateson relies on some ordinary understanding of the notion which he does not think necessary to specify.

Similarly, in *Right & Left* neither Evans-Pritchard nor the editor defines the word, and the other contributors equally employ it without deliberate gloss. The individual analyses provide ethnographic settings in which it seems appropriate, but only occasionally is there a hint at a specific sense. Thus in the study of symbolic classification among the Meru it is stated that "it is the *complementarity* . . . which should be emphasized, rather than differential status [of Mugwe and elders] in opposed contexts" (p. 117). Faron, writing about the relationship between Mapuche morality and its expression in various social institutions, suggests that "an integrating concept, such as complementary dualism," is needed (p. 191). Rigby, describing symbols and activities associated with men or with women among the Gogo, states that "the emphasis is upon the complementarity of the oppositions rather than their 'superiority' or 'inferiority'" (p. 267). Among the Nyoro, princess and diviner are seen as exemplifying "the complementary functions of secular power and mystical authority" (p. 316); more generally, "the rationale of Nyoro symbolic classification . . . is complementary dualism, and the defining term is opposition" (p. 326). Finally from this source, Middleton says of Lugbara concepts that they are "both opposed and complementary" (p. 372); "the complementarity of the pairs is a necessary one for the continuity of a divinely created and ordered cosmos" (p. 377).

A more or less tacit premise to the passages quoted is that opposites may or may not be complementary, and that when they possess what we have called connexity the link is provided by complementarity. But it is not at once clear, all the same, what it means for one opposite to be complementary to another. Until this is clarified we shall still have found no key to opposition in the quality of connexity.

IV

A standard definition of "complementary" is: completing, forming a complement. A complement is defined as: that which completes. The transitive verb "to complement" means: to complete. This set of senses expresses what is no doubt the ordinary understanding of the general idea of complementarity, and it does not get us very far. In order to get a better grasp on the notion, we need to survey some of the more particular acceptations of these words.

According to the *Oxford English Dictionary,* the noun "complement" has as its main meanings: the action of fulfilling or completing; the fact or condition of being complete; that which completes or makes perfect, the completion, perfection, consummation; the quantity or amount that completes or fills, complete quantity, provision, or set, full allowance, totality; the full number required to complete a company; something which, when added, completes or makes up a whole, each of two parts which mutually complete each other, or supply each other's deficiencies. There are also more special uses of the word: in mathematics, the two lesser parallelograms, not on the diagonal, made by drawing lines parallel to the sides of a given parallelogram, through the same point in its diagonal; in astronomy, the difference between the altitude, latitude, declination, etc., of a heavenly body, and 90 degrees; in navigation, so many points as the course wants of 90 degrees or eight points; in music, the interval which, together with any given interval, makes up a complete octave; in optics, that color which, mixed with another, produces white. A further main sense is: anything that goes to make up or fully equip; a completing accessory or adjunct. The adjective "complementary" means, in reference to the several senses of the noun: forming a complement, completing, perfecting; of two (or more) things, mutually complementing or completing each other's deficiencies. Complementary angles are those which together make up a right

angle. "Complementarity" is a relatively modern formation: in physics it designates (1928) the capacity of the wave
and particle theories of light together to explain all phenomena of a certain type, although each separately accounts for only some of the phenomena (Supplement, vol.
1, s.v.). It is not recognized in Lalande (1951) as a technical
term in philosophy, though Ayer writes that "two statements are complementary if and only if each is the negation of the other" (1954:61). In linguistics, a complementary distribution is that of two or more similar or related
speech-sounds or forms in such a manner that they appear
only in different environments.

The brief account above gives a fair idea of the range of
employment of words expressing complementarity, and
some indication of their common focus. Certain of the
glosses are of particular interest; for instance, "Justice and
Love are each the complement of the other"; "the animal
and the spiritual are . . . the complements in the perfect
character"; and also the notion, in nineteenth-century eco-
nomics, of "complementary goods" such as paper, pen,
and ink, needle and thread, cart and horse, bow and arrow.
These last examples especially are easily recognized as displaying a kind of connexity; we shall return below to the
grounds of the relation in such cases and in their bearing on
social facts.

The etymology of "complement" and its related forms
is quite direct. The word comes from the Latin *complēmen-
tum,* from *complēre,* to fill up, finish, fulfil (Onions 1966:
198); and from this same verb we have "complete," meaning entire, finished, perfect, accomplished, consummate.
Complēre, in its turn, is formed from *com-* as an inten-
sive, with the connotation of "altogether, completely," and
*ple-, the base of "full." This last word belongs to an ex-

tensive series of Indo-European words expressing fullness or abundance (p. 380, s.v.).

V

We are now in a position to return to the quality of complementarity as an aspect of opposition. From this point onward, however, we cannot assume that the diverse implications of this concept were at all present to the minds of those who have used the words "complementary opposites" in their ethnographic analyses. What we have to seek, rather, is what there is in the resources of the concept that might serve to elucidate the general feature of connexity between opposites.

To begin with, it is an interesting if slightly discouraging fact that complementarity has no standard use in symbolic logic. Unlike relations such as symmetry or transitivity (cf. Needham 1983:94), it is represented by no conventional sign or formula. It may prove convenient therefore to invent an abbreviation, at least, to stand for complementarity, namely: $/c/$. Thus $a/c/b$ will be read as a is complementary to b, and vice versa, or as a and b are complementaries. (An alternative and perhaps logically superior formula would be: $c(a/b)$. But the abbreviation proposed will serve, and for some readers it may display the form of the relationship rather more conveniently.) In ethnographic terms an example might be: priest$/c/$king. This example introduces a stipulation that needs to be made. The relation of complementarity (to the as yet hypothetical extent that it is a distinct mode of relation) is to be contrasted with that which obtains between correlatives. There are two reasons for this precondition. One is formal, namely that otherwise there might be no distinct use for the concept of complementarity. The other reason is pragmatic, namely that ethnographic practice has induced us to distinguish complementarity as a distinct kind of link between opposites, and it is this assumption that has to be tested. For illustrations of an apparent difference of kind between correlatives and complementaries, we may revert to the Kaguru opposites cited from Beidelman (above, sec. III). Red/white, we took it, is not an opposition of correlatives, and neither is sperm/blood; but the effect of Beidelman's analysis is that we can yet construe these oppositions as complementaries: red/c/white and sperm/c/blood. How far this is correct, or at any rate defensible, is a question that must wait upon a later development of the argument.

Apparently a distinguishing and essential feature of complementary opposites is that together they form a whole, something that is thereby complete. What does this mean? The standard definitions of "whole," as adjective and noun, include: in good health; in sound condition, intact; integral, consisting of one or more units; undiminished, without removal of parts; a thing complete in itself, all that there is in or of something, all members of. The etymology of the word goes back through (O)HG *heil* to Common Germanic *(ga)χailaz,* from IE *qoilos.* Philosophically, the concept of a whole was already taken up by Aristotle in the *Metaphysics,* and with his observations (in bk. Δ) we can begin to think analytically about this important but rather obscure idea.

Aristotle begins with the straightforward description that a whole is that which lacks none of those parts in virtue of which it is called a natural whole. A second definition is: that which contains its contents in such a way that they form a unity; there can be a variety of unities. The most consequential definition for our purposes is the third: "Since quantities have a beginning, a middle, and an end, those to which the position of their parts makes no difference are 'totals'; those to which it does are 'wholes'; and those to which it may or may not are both, for they have both characteristics" (1961:41). At another place (bk. Z), he takes up the crucial question, "Must the definition of the parts be present in that of the whole?" (1961:189). His immediate answer is: "It all depends." The definition of the circle does not include that of its segments, while that of the syllable does include that of its letters; and yet the circle is divisible into segments no less than the syllable into letters. A second consideration is that wholes are considered prior to their parts both in definition "(because the parts are explained by reference to them)" and in their power of independent existence. This leads Aristotle into the examination of what parts are nonetheless prior to the whole. This is a long matter, including the discrimination of an ideal form from a concrete whole and leading to essence, primary substances, and other notions that are not directly relevant to the present part of our investigation. Aristotle does, however, set us on the alert by starting with the assertion that the very word "part" is equivocal. His treatment of this point also involves metaphysical arguments that we may pass over here, but we may be arrested by his conclusion: "the definition of a whole will include that of the parts only if it refers to the concrete whole" (p. 190). It is of less importance that we grasp Aristotle's reasons for this conclusion, or what he advances as its consequences, than that we perceive its literal pertinence to our present problem.

There is of course much else, in other sources and authorities, that could be cited on the topics of whole and

part, but the above points taken from Aristotle are particularly suitable. In the first place they have his authority, and
they give a classical cast to the formulation of our special
problem, just as they have done to the terms in which it is
framed. In the second place they make an instructive contrast with Aristotle's treatment of opposites; for it is notable that just as "whole" and "part" are not mentioned in
that context (above, chap. 4), so his classification of opposites is not mentioned in connection with whole and
part. He does, of course, write about attributes that belong
to things, and about things that belong to genera, so that
the notions in question must be implied; but then it is
equally obvious that as much could be said about the treatment of anything that is a thing and is divisible. The present point, rather, is that the terms "whole" and "part" have
been accorded no formal use in the analysis of opposition.
This does not mean that there is no useful connection to be
made, for we have established that Aristotle's classification
of opposites is not well adapted to the analysis of opposites
such as have been described as complementary. But the
point just made is an indication, all the same, that if the
concepts of whole and part are implicit in complementary
opposition, as by definition they must be, then they contribute to this relation in some way not disclosed by even
Aristotle's analysis.

Ogden's analysis, on the other hand, with its diagrammatic dependence on the cut and the scale, directly invokes
in each instance of opposition the image of a whole that is
divided into parts. But his method has been found in numerous cases and respects to be unconvincing, and largely
in fact because of its reificatory premises and vocabulary. It
is also a fact, for that matter, that Ogden does not discuss
the general problems of whole and part, considered liter-

ally, in connection with the analysis of opposition. So if complementarity is somehow at work in the constitution of some kinds at least of opposition, it seems to have escaped Ogden's investigation also.

Tested against the ideas of our two exemplars, complementarity appears to be a rather evasive factor, if indeed that is what it is, and we need therefore to try to isolate it from different premises.

VI

The survey carried out above (sec. IV) registered an extensive range of use for the adjective "complementary," in many different undertakings and contexts, but no distinct employment was ascribed to it in the study of social facts.

It seems to have been taken up by anthropologists, perhaps in the main since the nineteen-fifties, for their own particular purposes but without a deliberate formulation of a precise sense appropriate to those purposes. In the study of dual symbolic classification especially, as represented in *Right & Left,* it has become prominent as a standard means of describing, or at any rate indicating, a common sort of opposition. What is still obscure, though, is what distinct purpose has been served by the allusion to "complementary" opposites in contrast with any other. A piecemeal way of clarifying this issue would be to carry out an exegesis of the term in its several contexts of ethnographic analysis; but this would be a long business, and it would amount to a cumulative and circumstantial account of accepted uses of the adjective, but no more. That is, although it could be instructive as an exercise in lexicography, it does not in itself seem likely to elicit whatever may be fundamental in complementary opposition. In order to do this we need to work out, as we have already intimated, an abstract scheme of complementarity.

The first question, from among those prompted by Aristotle, is whether complementary opposites together form a unity. The dictionary definition of a unity is that it is a complex whole made up of parts in due coherence and order, so it may appear that the question asks too much. But let us take it that what we want to know is merely whether the complementary terms constitute a unity in the sense of a singular entity. We need to ask this before we can consider whether it is a total or a whole. Well, if there is such a unity, it is one for which there need be no distinct name, and for which there appears ordinarily to be in fact no name. Consider one of the first dyads listed in table 2: above/c/below. These terms have already been characterized as correlatives (chap. 4, sec. III), and in this respect they possess connexity; that is, they belong together as a pair of attributes. We shall not yet ask what additional property they possess that would justify speaking of them as complementary. At present we have to decide first whether they constitute a unity. Their clear connexity and the definite relation between them would seem to make them a good case to be considered such. But if that is what they are, they are not singled out as a unity by the possession of a distinct name. They are connected by the fact that they are terms of relative location in the vertical dimension, but they are not known together as verticality, nor are they paradigmatic of that dimension. They represent one mode of connexity within the dimension, just as do top/bottom, but the connexity is premised on the irreducible fact that they are two and not a unity. Perhaps, though, this is too definite an example, such that the very clarity of its correlative constitution works against it being regarded as a unity. Let us therefore take another example from table 2, not of attributes this time, but things.

The dyad potted bloom/wild flower is composed of terms that can be seen as contraries; a taxonomic connection between them is that they are (let us assume; see chap. 4, sec. III) species of the genus flower. But all this means is that they can be classed together under the superior taxon of flower; the name of that taxon is not the name of the two of them considered together as a unity. Certainly they can be conceived as a dyad without being identified by a singular appellation, but they remain two things and not one; their connexity depends on their distinction as two things standing in a certain relationship. This relationship does not compose them into a unity except in the sense that they are conceived as a dyad, and also that as a dyad they can be distinguished from other dyads. Perhaps, however, such a mental conflation can itself qualify as a form of unity. After all, the interrelationship of the two things is not an objective property, and if they can be conceived together as opposites they can with equal justification be conceived as constituting a dyad, in other words as a compound unity.

Granted as much, we can go on to ask what kind of unity is composed by complementary opposites. According to Aristotle, when the position of the parts makes no difference we have a total, and when it does we have a whole. But the terms of our dyads, as in table 2, have no positions except on a printed line or within the coordinates of a diagram. Probably a conceptual unity with a greater number of parts could be better assessed by this criterion; for instance, a pair of contraries with an intermediate might be considered to form such a whole. But the terms of a dyad have, with respect to each other, no such formal posi-

tions. Even within the latitude afforded by the spatial metaphor of opposition, all that can be said is that they are opposites; but this does not confer on them any positions by
independent coordinates. They therefore do not qualify, by
Aristotle's criterion, as a whole; so in this sense they are not
complementary. They can perhaps be regarded, nevertheless, as composing a total, but it is not evident what we
shall have understood by doing so. Two numbers, when
added together, make up a total that is their sum, and it is a
different number, but these conditions do not obtain when
we consider complementary opposites. Take for example
the dyad right/c/left. If these two terms are to make up a
total, we have the implicit addition: right+left = (right+
left). But this is an ineffectual tautology, for there is no true
sum; the parentheses are simply a conventional means of
conveying that the terms enclosed by them are to be taken
together, in this case as a hypothetical total. This total,
however, is something we are trying to discover, not fab-
ricate with signs that beg the question. It cannot be contended, either, that right and left compose laterality, and
that this can be conceived as their total, for laterality is the
dimension within which they are necessarily defined, and
conversely they define the dimension, so that under this aspect as well there is a tautology. Nor is the vacuous outcome brought about by choosing a wrong sort of example,
for the result is essentially the same with black/c/white or
male/c/female or sun/c/moon. If the complementarity
that is ascribed by the sign /c/ has indeed any function, it is
not that the terms of the dyad compose a total, over and
above what is signified by their conjunction, and within
which each term is the complement of the other in producing that total.

To sum up, a complementary opposition forms a unity

only by stipulation; it is a conceptual artefact. The terms that are the parts of this unity do not combine to form a product of a higher order; it is only by the prior description of the dyad as a unity that each term, when related to the other, can be said to complement the other and thus to complete the opposition. The terms do not define a whole, nor yet a total, and they are not explained (to adopt Aristotle's word) by reference to a distinct entity of which they are the parts. The notion of a complete entity (the dyad as a compound unity) has sense here only in virtue of the relationship in which the one term stands to the other. It has not yet appeared that this relationship is usefully to be described as complementary.

VII

We have been trying to work out an abstract scheme of complementary opposition, but we have had to start from a nonabstract base; this is provided by the adjective "complementary," and we have been guided by its literal formation and by its common employment. In particular, we have been looking to see if connexity is to be explained by complementarity.

Now we can postulate without prejudice that dyads are discriminable as representations, and we can also propose that the terms of the dyads are linked by connexity, but we have failed to explain connexity by the factor of complementarity. Moreover, a return to the variety of uses served by this notion raises a matter that we have not so far considered. Even if it were feasible to justify the concept of opposites as complementary, still this mode of relation would not be exclusive to opposition. In fact, it is fairly easy to find instances of complementarity that are not oppositions. As the example of "complementary goods" shows (above, sec. IV), many pairs of things can be considered as complementary without being described as opposites. Such are: pen and ink, needle and thread, cart and horse, bow and arrow. In these examples, also, there is an evident principle at work: each thing is linked to its counterpart in a particular task to which both together are functionally necessary. Other examples of the kind would be: lock and key, knife and fork (also chopsticks, between which no lexical distinction is made), mortise and tenon, hammer and chisel, and so on. In the field of social functions, we can add: pilot and navigator (also, pilot and copilot), father and mother (which Ogden found difficult to handle as opposites), priest and king.

So the property of complementarity can certainly be recognized as qualifying the relationship between pairs of terms, and by this functional criterion it is possible in principle that certain oppositions could usefully be called complementary. But if we look at the thirteen dyads in table 2, we see that, although they can indeed conventionally be described as opposites, none of them is complementary in this functional sense. The list of Ogden's pairs of words (table 5), which he presents as opposites, similarly includes none that is complementary in this sense, with the possible exception of male/female; each of these latter terms is certainly necessary to the other in the task of sexual reproduction, though whether the connotations of the terms are also complementary, and in what range of further tasks, is a contingent question. It is possible that we could discover more instances of functional complementarity in ethnographic "tables of opposites," but these precisely would restate a fundamental difficulty that we have already registered. To identify such instances would demonstrate the incidence of functional complementarity among certain pairs of dyads, but this would not prove that the dyads were thereby opposites. Nor would it account for connexity, since we have already seen that established dyads need have nothing to do with functional complementarity, just as complementaries of this kind need have nothing to do with opposition.

There remains another acceptation of complementarity that should also be considered. We might say that the terms of a dyad were complementary if one of the terms evoked the other or if it acquired significance, or an added significance, in relation to the other. There are echoes here of Sir Thomas Browne declaring that contraries are the life of one another (1643, pt. 2, sec. 4), and of Swedenborg explaining that a thing cannot exist without its contrary (see Needham 1985:131). Perhaps in such a case the terms of a dyad could even be seen as complementing each other in the performance of a conceptual "task." How far this would be convincing would depend on distinguishing analysis from metaphor, as well as on the proper characteristics of the case considered. But there is in any event an objection of method. For one term to evoke another is to evince connexity, and it is a sufficient condition of connexity, without any need to imagine in addition a dyad carrying out a distinct task, by means of complementarity, the product of which would be the connexity. If entities are not to be multiplied beyond necessity, complementarity itself has no distinct function here. This much can be confirmed by considering again our table 2, in collation with table 4. The connexity of one of the dyads is accounted for by correlation, to which complementarity in the present sense is redundant, and the other dyads (with the one unclassified exception) are all adequately accounted for as contraries. Similar considerations would attach to the pairs of words in table 5, if with more complication because so much depends not on formal criteria but on connotations and values.

With such considerations we are inevitably implicated in semantic concerns that cannot adequately be treated by formal or abstract means of analysis. In the interpretation of mystical or of symbolic classifications, the vague phrase "complementary opposites" may then have a persuasive employment, of the sort that is appropriate to the translation of culture, even though neither word can strictly speaking be justified in the abstract. The concept of complementarity in particular, as it has been scrutinized here, has no intrinsic logical form (Needham 1985:162), and it possesses no formal properties such as might be defined in the notation of symbolic logic (contra Needham 1983:62). Instead, it can well be ascribed a more or less adventitious use as a term of expository rhetoric, especially in reference to values and symbols that do not readily yield to a more formal kind of systematic investigation. The word may then be exploited for the sake of practically any of the extensive variety of odd-job meanings that we have surveyed (sec. IV above), and no doubt such other senses as could be contrived in response to particular cases, but this accommodating utility would not constitute an essential or technical sense making it suitable for employment in comparative analysis. To the extent also that complementarity has been taken for a constituent of opposition, or as a significant aspect of it, the elision of the idea of "complementary" opposites in a formal sense must further detract from the standing of opposition as a distinct mode of relation.

Seven

Hierarchy

I note these defects without animadversion.

J. L. Borges

I

In the study of opposition there is currently a distinct approach, quite forcefully expressed, that we are now in a position to examine. It is focused on a peculiar form of complementarity that (with good reason) we have not so far encountered, and it presses for the recognition of a special mode of relation between part and whole. Its premises are deeply based, and in its particular contentions it poses unevadable challenges.

Louis Dumont has published two major critical articles that call into grave question the method of analyzing oppositions, as institutionalized in dual symbolic classification, that has become established during the greater part of

the present century. The articles are "La Communauté anthropologique et l'idéologie" (1978) and a Radcliffe-Brown
Lecture entitled "On Value" (1982). They have been re-
issued, the latter in French translation, in a collection of
Dumont's essays called *Essais sur l'individualisme* (1983,
chaps. 6 and 7). In the former article Dumont asserts that a
number of contemporary professional practices are "de-
structive" of the anthropological community (1978:100);
in the latter he claims that a certain approach to the analysis
of the opposition right/left, one that has prevailed from
Hertz (1909) down to the present day, is "wholly mistaken"
(1982:220). If these charges are justified, certain principles
of comparativism will have to be revised, and a new analytical vocabulary will have to be adopted.

An initial difficulty, however, in coming to terms with
this theory (let us call it) is that it is expressed in a manner
that is assertive yet recondite, abrupt in pronouncement yet
enigmatic in implication. This style of exposition makes
the argument difficult to follow with confidence and naturally that much harder to recount. Where Dumont is at his
most prolix, moreover, his precise meaning tends to become yet more obscure (see also Delfendahl 1973, pt. 2:
"Louis Dumont"), and this makes it difficult to sum up his
argument with much sureness that one is not misrendering
his thought. It might be feasible to participate more fully
in his outlook by tracing certain key words and ideas back
through his previous publications, but it cannot be our task
here to attempt so radical an exegesis. The subject of the
present monograph is opposition, with special reference to
dual symbolic classification, and Dumont's arguments will
be taken into account to the extent that they are relevant to
that end. This needs to be done in considerable detail, nonetheless, in order to allow Dumont, within reasonable lim-

its, to speak for himself. The degree of detail, moreover, will serve to support the argument of chapter 8 as well. The intricacy of Dumont's theory demands a careful recapitulation, and, even though the extent of our present concerns is quite specifically limited, this necessarily becomes the more complex as the argument advances. Yet, all the same, it is advisable first to try to grasp Dumont's premises and ideological predilections.

It ought to be possible to do justice to his approach, on all these scores, by concentrating on his latest pronouncements in the two publications cited above. Reference will be made to them individually, not to the volume in which they have more recently been incorporated, if only for the reason that the major article, that on value, was originally published in English. The volume will be cited, however, for the sake of its lexicon of key words (1983:263–64) in which Dumont provides concise definitions of what he presents as basic terms. The two articles are closely connected in theme, and there is significant overlap on the topic of the correct analysis of the opposition of right and left, so they will be considered together.

II

Dumont thinks that the social sciences are in a weak position because of their direct exposure to their ideological environment, and that this is fundamentally opposed—because it is individualistic—to the very principle of anthropology and of any sound and fundamental sociology. Anthropology is fragmented, moreover, and in the present generation it proliferates "pseudoanthropologies" which are tantamount to "antianthropologies." Dumont, by contrast, holds to "the true nature of anthropology," of which one of the alluring characteristics is its ambition to transcend specialities and its promise of "an access to totality" (1978:84–85). Here we see introduced, in a professional setting, the major themes of individualism and totality, together with Dumont's aversion from the former and his aspiration toward the latter.

The modern ideology at work is the set of common representations that are "*characteristic*" of modern civilization. (An ideology in general is a social set of representations, or of ideas and values common to a society, and also a specified part of such a global ideology, such as the economic ideology.) Individualism is opposed to holism as an ideology that places value on the individual and neglects or subordinates the social totality; holism is an ideology that places value on the social totality and neglects or subordinates the individual human being. Totality is not separately defined (1983, Lexique).

The opposition between individualism and holism is solidary with that between modern and "nonmodern" societies. We can take modern societies to be typified by those of Europe and the Americas, but the opposed type is scarcely indicated by the negation, and one is left to compose its character by means of various attributes dispersed throughout the texts. There is no concise definition or illustration of the nonmodern, but Dumont seems to have in mind traditional India and such societies as those of Melanesia (1982:225). There is a most important difference between the two types of society with regard to value: the modern ideology separates values and facts, whereas other ideologies "embed values in their world view" (1982:219). In the former type (i.e., modern), some of the values, instead of emanating from the society, will be determined by the individual for his own use; freedom of conscience is the standard example. Contrariwise, and very generally (i.e., in nonmodern societies), value is embedded in the configuration of ideas, and this condition prevails so long as the relation between part and whole is effectively present, so long as experience is spontaneously referred to degrees of totality.

So there are two alternative configurations: either value attaches to the individual (modern) or it attaches to the whole in relation to its parts (nonmodern) (1982:232–33). Concomitantly, there are two conceptions or definitions of a whole: one through a rigid boundary, the other through internal dependence and consistency; "the former is modern and arbitrary or somewhat mechanical, the second traditional and structural" (1982:226–27). As a contingent but congruent observation, Dumont asserts that "relational analysis demands that the boundaries of the 'system' be rigorously defined" (1982:208 n. 1).

This preamble may seem to have no bearing on the analysis of the concept of opposition, let alone a specific opposition, yet on the contrary it establishes premises and conclusions that are essential (or at any rate Dumont must think they are) to that task. The connection is to be made via Dumont's notion of "hierarchy." Near the beginning of his lecture on value, he states his position: "I have been trying in recent years to sell the [anthropological] profession the idea of hierarchy, with little success" (1982:208). Some of this lack of success, we are given to understand, is a result of the egalitarianism that is characteristic of our modern ideology and that makes hierarchy "decidedly unpopular" (1978:101). In the nonmodern view, however, the value of an entity is dependent upon or intimately related to "a hierarchy of levels of experience" in which that entity is situated; this is perhaps the main perception that moderns miss or ignore or suppress, so that in modern ideology "the previous hierarchical universe" is fanned out into a collection of "flat views" (1982:223, 222). This precisely is held to underlie the unsatisfactory nature of recent analyses of the opposition of right and left. But before this issue can be considered it is necessary to collate the main senses in which "hierarchy" is used by Dumont, and, together with these, the meaning he ascribes to "level."

A compendious definition of hierarchy, in the first article cited, relates to opposition: hierarchic opposition is "*encompassment of the contrary* [englobement du contraire] as type of relation between element and ensemble" (1978: 101); the element is not necessarily simple, and it can be a sub-set (*sous-ensemble*). (It is hard to find in English a precise equivalent to the French *ensemble,* which is not all that precise anyway. In some contexts, "totality" will serve, and also in distinction to Fr. *tout,* whole, a word that Dumont differentiates from *ensemble.* There is perhaps a derivation from Aristotle here; see above, chap. 6, sec. V.) An opposition of this kind is analyzable logically into contradictory partial aspects: on the one hand, the element is identical with the ensemble to the extent that it forms part of it; on the other hand, there is a difference or more strictly contrariety (p. 103). This is called a "logical scandal," yet every relation of a part to the totality of which it forms part introduces hierarchy and is thus logically unacceptable. This, it is suggested, explains the disfavor with which it is viewed and at the same time makes it interesting (p. 104).

These statements, as they stand, may not appear to be perspicuous, and their coherence is not easily evident, but they are considerably developed or elaborated in the second of the texts under examination. An early use of the word "hierarchy" is at a place where Dumont writes of a hierarchy between conception and operation, a phrase which in the next line is rephrased as "distinction between the two levels" (1982:211). This also is not perfectly clear, but it has its value as illustrating Dumont's equivalences of idiom and also as an example of hierarchy apart from opposition (unless, what is not stipulated, conception and operation are taken as opposites). More generally, "where non-moderns distinguish levels within a global view, the moderns know only of substituting one special plane of consideration for another, and find on all planes the same forms of neat disjunction, contradiction, etc." (pp. 211–12). There are also "levels of social life," and Dumont regards it as "characteristic of modern artificialism to disregard such levels altogether" (p. 218). This is followed immediately by the assertion that, in Dumont's opinion, there is actually a "need" to reintroduce "some measure of holism into our individualistic societies."

Dumont lays special stress on the fact that values are intimately combined with nonnormative representations; a system of values is hence an abstraction from a wider system of "ideas-and-values" (1982:220). These are complex entities, and difficult to handle; they are multidimensional, and to grasp them in their interrelations "goes against our most ingrained habits." Yet there are three characteristics through which they can be approached. First, idea-values are ranked. Second, this ranking "includes reversal as one of its properties." Third, the configuration is normally segmented (1982:224).

It is necessary for us to try to grasp something of these matters if we are to understand Dumont's treatment of the right/left opposition. First, ranking: it is explained that "high" ideas will both contradict and include "low" ideas;

"an idea that grows in importance and status acquires the property of encompassing its contrary" (p. 225). An illustration is a Melanesian system of exchanges, such as prestations and goods; "I mean prestations (relations between men) including things or encompassing their contrary, things." Another example is that of the "hierarchical opposition" of good and evil; "good must contain evil while still being its contrary" (p. 224). In other words, it is explained, real perfection is not the absence of evil but its perfect subordination; a world without evil could not possibly be good. As for reversal: Dumont instances what he calls "the logical relationship" between priest and king, as in India or in early Christianity; "in matters of religion, and hence absolutely, the priest is superior to the king . . . to whom public order is entrusted," but "the priest will obey the king in matters of public order, that is, in subordinate matters" (p. 225). Dumont calls this a chiasmus that is characteristic of hierarchy of the articulate type. To this we can subjoin a previous comment about what he takes for a universal phenomenon; this is a "characteristic complementarity or reversal between levels of experience where what is true on the more conceptual level is reversed on the more empirical level" (p. 211). In general, also, the moment the second function is defined, it entails the reversal of the situations belonging to it; "hierarchy is *bidimensional,* it bears not only on the entities considered but also on the corresponding situations, and this bidimensionality entails the reversal" (p. 225). As for segmentation: "value is normally segmented in its application, except in specifically modern representations." For example, in India distinctions are variably stressed according to the situation at hand, whereas "we think mostly in black and white, extending over a wide range of clear either/or disjunctions and using a small number of rigid, thick boundaries defining solid entities" (p. 226).

III

If there is much in this catalogue of contrastive assertions that seems baffling, it may be that a clearer import and coherence will emerge from a specific instance of analysis. This is found in Dumont's treatment of dual symbolic classification and, in particular, the opposition of right and left. This topic is presented as example, the only one to be examined in detail, in both of the articles.

Dumont opens the case by affirming the necessity of universal concepts within the research community. Failing substantive elements, such universals will be types of relations. One of these is "distinctive opposition"; this is not defined, though its acquisition is said to be fundamental. It is necessary, however, to add to this type that of "hierarchic opposition or *encompassment of the contrary* as type of the relation between element and totality." Dumont observes here that, having introduced this opposition elsewhere, he would readily have left to others the fairly obvious task of applying it—but this was not done. So he proposes to defend and illustrate hierarchic opposition by reference to a case in which distinctive opposition is not enough. This turns out to be the collective volume *Right & Left,* a work so replete with allusions to opposition that this word finds no place in the index (Needham, ed. 1973). It is selected as being representative of a type of analysis (Dumont 1978: 102).

Even if we entertain the assumption that there actually is a single type of analysis that is common to the eighteen chapters that make up the book, Dumont does not very accurately identify its premises or its method. He reports that the symbolic system, or in his word the ideology, is considered in itself and more or less independently of the social morphology; "what is curious . . . is that the Evans-Pritchardian distinction of situations should be neglected" (1978:102). What may be thought rather more curious is that these matters are in fact explicitly taken into account by the authors throughout the course of the book.

Social morphology is the foundation of La Flesche's study, for instance; he begins with "the complex organization of the tribe," and he sets the scene for his analysis by means of a diagram of the dual organization of the Osage (*Right & Left:* 32, 33). Granet's essay on China has to do with the very general issue of etiquette as an expression of the structure of the world (p. 44), and it is packed with specific social situations of many different kinds. So much is this so that when Dumont himself conjectures a hierarchic articulation such as might reintroduce holism into modern society, he twice cites as a parallel "the highly elaborate Chinese etiquette" (1982:218, 239). Likewise, Kruyt, writing about Celebes, describes one social situation after another, including mourning, weddings, harvesting, and warfare; if there is little explicitly on social morphology, there is still repeated emphasis on the distinction of situations. If Dumont means his criticism to apply to the more recent authors, the fact is that these are even less open to the charge of neglecting the social setting. Certainly he could not intend to include Evans-Pritchard's own essay on the Nuer under his stricture. The chapter on the Meru proposes certain correlations (what they are worth is another matter) between symbolic representations and types of descent system, and it stresses Meru patriliny; the analysis takes as central the functions of the Mugwe in relation to Meru social divisions, and it concentrates on this society as an instance of dual sovereignty. Beidelman contends expressly that Kaguru symbolic classification is "closely related to certain aspects of Kaguru social structure" (1973: 131), and he demonstrates as much.

It would be wearisome to extend the refutation by quoting additional allusions to social morphology or situations in the essays by Faron, Cunningham, Rigby, Littlejohn, the editor (on the Nyoro this time), Fox, Middleton, and Beck. It can, however, be maintained that the emphasis on the social setting of dual symbolic classification actually becomes more marked in the course of the book, culminating with Beck's examination of right-hand and left-hand castes as constituting the "division of South Indian society." An important point of method, moreover, is that author after author abstracts the symbolic system deliberately from the social morphology and by the distinction of situations.

IV

On the score of method, also, Dumont has apparently lapsed into another misunderstanding of that which he castigates, and this too needs to be cleared away before we can consider the merits of his own method.

He remarks on the common premises that man thinks by distinctions, and that the resulting "oppositions" form some kind of system. Then he writes that the authors in *Right & Left* have thus been led to present lists of oppositions that are more or less homologous among themselves as binary classifications, or alternatively as "a sort of dualist grid containing the essential of the indigenous 'symbolic system,' or at least an important aspect of this system." This makes up a series of oppositions presented in two columns, as in the present table 6. Taken minimally, there is discovered in certain contexts what Dumont calls a "homology," represented by him as $a/b=e/f$; likewise, in another context, $e/f=i/k$. Dumont acknowledges the concern, expressed in *Right & Left,* that each of the oppositions should be taken in its context, or rather, as he puts it, that each of the homologies between two of these oppositions should be taken in its context. "But," he continues, "it is clear that in the construction of the table in two columns all the contexts are confused or elided" (1978:102).

In sum, he asserts, the distinction of situations ceases to be considered as soon as the passage to the totality (*ensemble*) is made, as though each situation in itself were independent of the totality of the "mentality," whereas it ought to be plain that the very distinction of the situations depends on the mentality in question. Dumont concedes that such "simplifications" are current when a new perspective is worked out, but he wonders whether this instance has been rectified elsewhere. "Nowhere do I see a systematic of the situations as they are classed, and thus defined, in the ideology under study. On the contrary, it is supposed, rather, that the ideological system is all of a piece, monolithic" (p. 103). At the end of his article he repeats the assertion that binary classification is insufficient: "it confuses uniformly contexts or situations which may or may not be distinguished in the ideology studied." Traditional China classified into two classes of symbols under the emblems of *yin* and *yang;* and in general "it can be said that this book [*Right & Left*] proceeds rather as though all the world were Chinese."

TABLE 6
Dualist Grid (Dumont)

a	*b*
e	*f*
i	*k*
o	*p*

Again, there has somehow opened up a serious discrepancy between what is written by the authors in question and what Dumont represents them as saying, and there is also some uncertainty already as to his own conception of the matters at issue. To begin with, what Dumont calls a homology would normally be described as an analogy; thus Lloyd has described how the philosophies of the Pythagoreans and of Heraclitus contain general doctrines which depend on "the recognition of an *analogy* . . . between the relationships between pairs of opposites of many different sorts" (1966:99, cf. 96). In the present instance, we have the proportional analogy $a : b :: e : f$ (a is to b as e is to f), or in other words a/b is analogous to e/f. That is, there is an analogy between the one relation of opposition and the other. In this connection, incidentally, we need not for the present lay much stress on Dumont's use of the equation sign (as in $a/b = e/f$), except to remark that it presumes an equality that in real terms has been proved not to obtain (see below, chap. 9, sec. VIII). A relation of homology, on the other hand, can be posited of individual terms; for instance, in table 6 the terms in one column are formally homologous one with another. Among them, a significant similarity between any two terms may be discernible in the ideology, giving a homology of the type $a \equiv e$ (cf. Needham 1973:xxviii; Needham, in Hocart 1970:xlvi–ix). Dumont does not define homology, and his example serves merely to intimate the sense he gives the word. For our purposes, with an eye to the later exposition, it may be helpful to keep in mind the sense of "homologous" as employed of chemical compounds: a series with constant successive differences of composition (cf., in table 6, b, f, k, p). At this point, it can perhaps be suggested that, by so departing from the conventions followed in the work he criticizes, Dumont has unfortunately introduced a gratuitous source of miscomprehension.

But this lapse is almost insignificant by comparison with his misrepresentation of what is implied by a table with two columns of opposites. The gravamen is that by the very construction of the table all the contextual distinctions are elided or confused. But this is to ignore, to begin with, the express caution uttered in *Right & Left* (pp. xxiv–v):

A two-column scheme, listing the oppositions in what is analyzed as a dual symbolic classification, is not a total and systematic depiction of a complete body of thought and imagery. It is a mnemonic and suggestive device which simply brings together in a convenient and apt fashion the series of oppositions that have been established; and these are usually listed . . . simply in the order in which they make their appearance in the course of the analysis. In itself the scheme neither states nor implies any boundaries or liaisons other than those that have been demonstrated. It is, to repeat this crucial point, no more than an expository convenience: a conventional figure that helps one to recall the cumulative effect of the argument.

It is this carefully qualified recourse to a mnemonic figure that Dumont describes as a passage to the totality of the mentality under study, and as a dualist grid constituting the essential of the symbolic system.

The qualifications just quoted are directly followed,

moreover, by the explicit statement that it is not suggested that a binary scheme of the kind in question exhibits a "total" character, based on the division of all the things and qualities listed into two opposed and mutually exclusive spheres; "this is certainly not so," the explication continues, and equally certainly it is not suggested by the form of the table that all of the things or qualities listed in each of the columns are thought to belong to a single category (p. xxv).

This is what Dumont describes as the confusion or elision of all the contexts. Here also is a miscomprehension that might have been thought sufficiently guarded against, and all the more when the fallacious reading responsible is then averted in advance, in *Right & Left,* by two pages of demonstration (pp. xxv–xxvii) of "the overriding importance of context." This is what Dumont reports as: "the distinction of situations ceases to be considered pertinent" (1978:103).

Actually, in the volume under discussion, it is Hertz who says of homologous terms (such as sacred power, source of life, truth, beauty, virtue, the rising sun, the male sex, the right side) that they "are all interchangeable, as are their contraries; they designate under many aspects a single category of things, a common nature" (Hertz 1973:14). This idea is abjured, however, not only in the introduction to *Right & Left* but also by one author after another in the body of the text. For example, in the Meru analysis "it has to be kept in mind that the ascription of terms to one series in the scheme [of two columns] does not entail that they all share the particular attributes of any one term"; "the association rests on analogy" (p. 117). Beidelman, in his Kaguru analysis, carefully explains that the terms and connections of the symbolic classification that he has elicited are grasped to varying degrees by the Kaguru, and he thinks it very doubtful whether any individual Kaguru sees these various oppositive attributes as forming a single system (p. 154). There is all the less ground, therefore, to infer that the various distinct contexts of the terms in one column of the table are neglected or flattened out. Faron presents Mapuche oppositions in three separate tables, according to the generic contexts and preponderant values. Rigby stresses the "relativity" of the relations of right and left, good and bad, among the Gogo, and he appends to his table of two columns the comment, "it is evident that the ascription of certain terms to one or other of the series is surrounded by ambiguity in some contexts" (pp. 266, 280). As a final example, Middleton declares at the beginning of his analysis of dual classification among the Lugbara: "it is of little value merely to list examples of such a widespread phenomenon apart from their cultural contexts." Furthermore, he lists the paired elements in three separate series, according to their preponderant concerns and also as distinguished by their degrees of explicitness for the Lugbara (pp. 369, 386–87). This is what Dumont characterizes as a "dualist grid" in which each situation is represented as though it were independent of the mentality as a totality.

All of these are matters of textual fact, and they are settled (even if it is a tedious affair to do so) by going back to the sources in question. But what is not at all easily settled is the underlying problem as Dumont sees it. He asserts that by the construction of the standard table "all" of the cultural contexts are confused or elided. It is exceedingly hard to see how this result could possibly come about. What the analyst does is to focus on a situation that he finds interesting in the light of certain theoretical concerns; he analyzes this situation as the expression of an ideological opposition; then he enters the definitive terms in the table. In the scheme of the two columns, each pair of terms refers back to the context from which it was abstracted. None of the contextual analyses is vitiated thereby, but each one stands in the text and continues to make its own contribution to the argument; none is elided, and none is confused with any other. Yet Dumont insists that "it is clear" that this is actually the outcome. Perhaps a tendentious critic could take the table for the argument, but then he could not be understanding what the terms represented. In this way the contexts might somehow be confused or elided—but only in the mind of the critic, not in the analysis.

Even this seems improbable, however, if we just look at real cases. Take the dyads in table 2 as an example. How could the respective contexts of imaginary/concrete and flower/weed be confused? Or ethereal/terrestrial with cat/dog? Or, to compare dyads that are more alike, flower/weed with potted bloom/wild flower? To confuse is to mix things up in the mind, and in each of these instances to do so would mean neglecting their distinctive attributes in favor of others that they might or might not possess. This may be vaguely imaginable, but a real case for the danger of confusion would have to exemplify it in the precise particulars of a factual proposition, and this is precisely what Dumont does not provide. Yet he does contend that *all* of the contexts are confused or elided by the very construction of the table.

If the example of table 2 is objected to, as based on a fiction, take the opposites in table 5, which are vouched for by English usage. How could the respective contexts of black/white and open/shut possibly be confused? Or black/white with any of the remaining dyads? Or, at the limit, any dyad at all with any other? In the context of the table, the terms carry distinctive sense in connection with the several analyses that Ogden presents in detail; one reason for focusing on these terms is that they are different one from another, and in many cases so different that they could hardly be compared, let alone be confused. This indeed may have been a deliberate choice on Ogden's part, for then the comparative analysis in terms of cut and scale may appear all the more effective.

Finally, if even this example is objected to, as being contrived by the lexicologist, take any of the two-column tables in *Right & Left* and it will be seen how inconceivable it is that construction of the table should by itself confuse the respective contexts of the terms. If it is conceivable, Dumont does not tell us how it is done. And as for the alleged elision of the contexts: this charge can be correct only in the trivial sense that the terms stand for their several contexts but do not replicate them. Otherwise the charge of elision, as a result of the form of the table, makes no sense.

In the end, then, it is not merely that Dumont fails to register "the importance of keeping the context of opposition perpetually in view" (*Right & Left*: xxvii), but that the fallacious consequences that he warns against cannot even be realized. Of course, it is possible to draw mistaken inferences from a table of two columns, but that is a different matter, and then too it is possible only by "disregarding the crucial factor of context" (p. xxv)—which is entirely inconsonant with the principles of analysis on which such tables are based.

V

When Dumont criticizes adversely the work of his colleagues on dual symbolic classification, he may be mistaken, but this does not invalidate his positive contentions about what ought to be done instead. This is where the premises outlined in section II above become directly relevant.

He sets out to apply the "hierarchic principle" to binary classifications, or more precisely to the opposition between right and left that serves as their emblem (1978:104). This problem, as it appears in the literature and in *Right & Left,* is, he says, "essentially epistemological": the opposition is treated uniformly as a distinctive opposition, a simple polarity or complementarity. "But in fact the two terms or poles *do not have* an equal status: one (generally the right) is superior, the other inferior." Hence the problem as it has traditionally been posed: "How is it that the two opposites that we (gratuitously) take for equals are not such in reality?" Why the preeminence of one of the hands? What is missing here, Dumont continues, is the recognition that the right/left pair cannot be defined in itself, "but *only in relation to a whole,* a very concrete whole [*tout*] since what is in question is the human body." The fact is familiar to the physicist, who in order to be able to speak of right and left puts an imaginary observer in place (p. 105).

Then Dumont takes a crucial step: "To say that the right/ left opposition refers to a whole means that it has a hierarchic aspect." We are accustomed, he says, to analyzing this opposition in such a way as to separate fact (the presumed symmetry) from value (the added asymmetry). However, "concretely, in reality, right and left *are not in the same relation to the whole of the body,*" that is, to the whole that is the body. Thus they are differentiated in value at the same time as they are differentiated in nature. "The preeminence is not contingent here, but necessary, for it results from the differentiation of the two terms in relation to the whole." This conception of the matter, Dumont explains, in substituting an asymmetric opposition for "an imaginary symmetric opposition," or one of equal statuses, gets us closer to the thought that we are studying. We also rid ourselves of the needless difficulty that we create by separating facts (or ideas) and values (p. 106).

This much of a summary provides a fair idea of Dumont's main contentions concerning part and whole, asymmetry, and the all-important hierarchy. Before we consider the cogency of these contentions, however, we have to introduce another crucial component of his theory. This is the notion of "level" (*niveau*), in combination with that of reversal (1978 : 106).

By definition, a symmetric opposition is reversible at will: its inversion produces nothing. To the contrary, the inversion of an asymmetric opposition is meaningful; the inverted opposition *is not the same* as the initial opposition. If the inverted opposition is found in the same whole in which the direct opposition was present, it evidently indicates a *change of level*.

As a fine example of this arrangement, Dumont cites a description of the Kabyle house: once the threshold is crossed, space is turned round and the points of orientation are interchanged; it is as though the threshold were a center of symmetry between external space and the internal space of the house, which is inverted in relation to the former. Dumont sums up the lesson of this example by writing, "we have passed from one level of life to another" (p. 107).

Now the same thing is true, it is maintained, of right and left: "If, in passing from an element classified as left, preeminence is inverted, this indicates that this level is clearly distinguished from others in the indigenous ideology." Thus, it is claimed, a hierarchic apprehension of an opposition such as that between right and left directs us to the "distinction of levels in the global ideology." Whereas in binary classification (that is, as practiced by anthropologists in their analyses) distinctive opposition atomizes the data at the same time as it makes them uniform, hierarchic opposition reunites them by fusing two dimensions of distinction: between levels, and within a single level. The hierarchy of levels results from the very nature of ideology (p. 107), and hypothetically is a universal feature (p. 108). A grave inadequacy of binary classification (N.B., again, that produced by the anthropologist) is that it says nothing about this feature, and that it reduces to the same oversimple form the simplest as well as the most complex of these hierarchies. Perhaps it is in reference to the alleged inadequacy that Dumont alludes to "simple oppositions badly subsumed" (1982:237 n. 2 from 236).

Dumont concludes by stating that "binary classification" is insufficient from two points of view. So far as the oppositions themselves are concerned, the procedure wrongly takes to be of equal status oppositions that are not so, and it claims to grasp the anatomy of ideas independently of the values that are indissolubly attached to them. (This, by the way, is the fault of a "misplaced egalitarianism.") Secondly, the method confuses uniformly contexts and situations that may or may not be distinguished in the ideology studied.

Dumont's lecture on value, finally, cites the above argument in stressing the inseparability of ideas and values, and in stating that "reference to the body as to a *whole* to which right and left hands belong is constitutive of the right, the left and their distinction" (1982:220). He does, however, add a curious gloss: "The contention should be obvious: take a polar opposition at random, add to it a difference in value, and you will not get right and left. Right and left, having a different relation to the body . . . are different *in themselves*" (pp. 220–21). After then repeating the assertion that the relation between part and whole is hierarchic, Dumont concludes: "Thus the hands and their tasks or functions are at one and the same time different and ranked."

VI

The textual part of an appreciation of Dumont's argument is fairly straightforward in practice, if puzzling in effect. His opening and emphatic contention is that right and left are not of equal status, whereas the contributors to *Right & Left* are represented as putting them on a par by means of a merely "distinctive" opposition; they presume the two sides of the body to be equal and are then faced with the problem that in fact the sides are of unequal value.

Reading this account of the matter, one may be inclined to wonder if there is not perhaps some special sense to the words as Dumont uses them, or whether there is not some hidden meaning that one has failed to grasp, for in the ordinary way what he writes does not correspond at all to what his predecessors and colleagues have actually written. Every single author, in fact, starts from the basic datum that the values attached to the sides are unequal, not equal. Hertz's opening lines, in his classic essay, are: "What resemblance more perfect than that between our two hands! And yet what a striking inequality there is!" (1973:3). Certainly there is an anatomical resemblance, in that the hands are enantiomorphs of each other. (This means, incidentally, that they could resemble each other more, and perhaps even perfectly: this would be if they were not enantiomorphs, so that a person would have two "left" hands or two "right" hands.) But Hertz's essay is not about anatomy: it is about values, and, in this case, strikingly unequal values. The same is true of all the other essays in *Right & Left:* the common theme throughout is that of unequal lateral values and their distinctive symbols. The only place at which an equality of the hands is alluded to is where Hertz mentions the possibility that the disparity between them might be reduced by ambidextrous education in assuring "a more harmonious development of the organism" (p. 22). This expresses a hypothetical ideal for humanity, not an assumption that in reality the hands are equal; and the very premise of the ideal is the fact that right and left are unequal, so even this passage cannot be what Dumont has in mind.

We are left, therefore, to conjecture what he could possibly intend by his paradoxical account of the fundamental premise of all research carried out so far. Possibly it has something to do with his idea that the problem of right and left, as previously conceived, is essentially epistemological. This cannot in fact be the answer, however, for, as Dumont elsewhere concedes (1978:102), the interest of *Right & Left* is directed toward symbolic systems; and even if it were correct that the problem was taken to be epistemological, it still would not follow that researchers should treat right and left as forming a "distinctive" opposition. As we have noted, Dumont does not define this term, but he instantiates it as "simple 'polarity' or 'complementarity'." This does not help, either, for Lloyd demonstrated abundantly, in 1966, that polarity is by no means simple, and we have seen that complementarity is even less so. Nor, in any case, does either of these concepts commit the researcher to the idea that the terms of an opposition are, or should be, of equal status. The only simple aspect of this matter is the fact that those whom Dumont criticizes on these scores do not say what he says they say. But one would like to understand, all the same, why he thinks they do. Perhaps a clue is to be found in another charge that he prefers.

What others have missed, Dumont thinks, is the recognition that the right/left pair cannot be defined in itself, but only in relation to a whole, and specifically the concrete whole that is the human body. It is important to try to understand just what Dumont is saying here, for it not only has to do with part and whole but it directly implicates the notion of hierarchy.

To begin with, then, it is a truism that the opposition right/left cannot be defined in itself: the terms can be defined only in relation to something else. But it is not true that they can be defined only in relation to something that constitutes a whole. The arbitrary stipulation of a point of reference, combined with a given point of observation, is perfectly sufficient. The point of reference could be a map reference in a featureless desert, or the beam of a flashlight in a dark enclosure, or coordinates in space. In each instance, once the point of reference was established, the observer, at the given point of observation, could determine right and left, and without reliance on anything that could be called a whole.

If, all the same, we entertain Dumont's supposition that the opposition right/left does refer to the human body, still it does not follow that this must mean the body as a whole. Littlejohn, in considering the grounds for the distinction of right and left, nicely establishes that all that is needed, in reference to the human body, is the concept of a median line, and the characteristics he ascribes to this line are entirely adequate to the distinction (Littlejohn 1973:289). It is true that internal organs may constitute material points of reference along this line, as they do for the Temne, but this is a contingent matter of cultural fact and is not essential to the purpose. In this case also, therefore, there need be no whole.

If, nevertheless, we go on to entertain Dumont's assertion that right and left do refer to the concrete whole that is the human body, it is a question what sort of a whole he supposes this to be. Dumont adheres, it will be recalled (above, sec. II), to a distinction between two types: one defined by a rigid boundary, the other by internal dependence and consistency. A "concrete whole" sounds like the former type, but this is a "modern" conception, so presumably it is not what Dumont will have had in mind. The type defined by internal dependence, on the other hand, is "nonmodern," so it would seem that this is what he should intend. But what is unclear, in this case, is wherein the internal dependency consists. Ex hypothesi, the vectors of right and left are mutually dependent within the body, but it is these very distinctions that are to be accounted for by their dependence on other features, and what these may be has not been stated. We could guess, of course, but what we are meant to be engaged in here is a rational argument.

Dumont's resort to a concrete whole, in explaining the opposition of right and left, is therefore unfounded, but it is evidently important to him to assume the position he adopts. The purpose cannot be to claim that right and left are parts of this whole, for abstract concepts cannot form part of a concrete entity. Yet Dumont emphasizes that "concretely, in reality" right and left are not (respectively) in the same relation to the whole that is the body (1978: 105). This is directly followed by the assertion that "they are thus differentiated in value." There is no logical connection here, but the statement does serve to bring into conjunction the idea of a whole and that of value, and this leads to the conclusion: "as soon as different associations and functions are attached to them [right and left], this difference is hierarchic because it is related to a whole" (p. 105). At this point, therefore, we have to try to gain a critical purchase on Dumont's conception of hierarchy. This is not a straightforward task, in the case of this particular opposition, for he starts by saying in a qualified way that right/left has "a hierarchic aspect" and that it does not at first sight fall under the simple type of hierarchic opposition; but he nevertheless goes on to state that a lateral preeminence is not contingent but necessary, in that it results from the differentiation of the two terms in relation to the whole— which would seem by definition to argue after all for a hierarchic opposition. Let us then focus on the notion of hierarchy, in order to establish a main part of what the assertions above are supposed to mean.

The statement that "the relation between part and whole is hierarchic" (1982:221) implies that it is possible for a hierarchy to obtain, in Dumont's view, between only two terms. This is confirmed when he remarks that Koestler stresses hierarchy as "a chain of levels," whereas he himself insists on "the elementary relation between two successive levels" (p. 222, n. 1). Disregarding the extension of each of the terms, it thus appears that merely a difference of value between two terms (for example, right and left) constitutes a "hierarchy." This is a surprisingly unusual use of the word. Let us go back to what it normally means. The etymology (sacred rule) does not help directly, though Wyclif distinguished three orders of angels, and an ecclesiastical hierarchy is divided into more ranks than that. Lalande defines *hiérarchie* as "serial subordination," which implies more than two ranks. Robert has: "organization of a whole [*ensemble*] into a series in which each term is superior to the following term, by a characteristic of a normative nature" (1966:487). The *Trésor* gives as the usual sense: "social organization establishing relations of subordination and of graduated degrees of powers, situations, and responsibilities" (1981:832). The standard meaning of the French word thus corresponds to what is ordinarily understood by it in English: a hierarchy is an organization of grades or classes ranked one above another in a series.

It is odd, therefore, to find Dumont using this word to denote, as in the present instance, a mere difference of evaluation between no more than two terms; and it may seem odder still to describe the difference between conception and operation as a "hierarchy" (1982:211). But the matter becomes even more perplexing when Dumont comes to define the word in his lexicon (1983:263). Hierarchy is introduced there as the order resulting from the putting into play of value, and there are two types of it: (1) the elementary hierarchical relation (or: hierarchic opposition) is that between a whole (or: a totality) and an element of this whole or totality; (2) that between two parts in reference to the whole. Hierarchy is thus analyzed into "two contradictory aspects of different level: distinction within an identity, [and] *encompassment of the contrary*"; this is what is meant by saying that hierarchy is "bidimensional."

What Dumont has done, then, is to take a standard (if somewhat resonant) word and give it an idiosyncratic employment; this contrived meaning, moreover, is split into two distinct senses that are represented as mutually contradictory, even though these senses are those ascribed to the word by their fabricator. Whether these latter senses are really contradictory is questionable, but a resolution is hard to determine since we are here in the domain of a private vocabulary which may at any point confound our understanding of ordinary words. So let us take these distinctions as they stand, in order to see what use, if any, can be made of them.

A hierarchic opposition is, to be summary but sufficiently exact, that between part and whole. Dumont illustrates this by saying that on the one hand the part is "identical" to the whole (a vertebrate is an animal), and that on the other there is a contrariety (a vertebrate is not only an animal, and an animal is not necessarily a vertebrate) (1978: 103). This is the "double relation" that he describes as a logical scandal (above, sec. II). But it is nothing of the kind, and it can appear as such only because of a lax use of logical terms. On the former count, it is an illicit use of "identical" to say that a part of anything is identical with the genus under which it is subsumed. Also, a consequence of the identity of two things or terms is that one can be substituted for the other in a proposition, without a change of logic or significance; but, to take Dumont's example, there is no such equivalence between vertebrate and animal, so that one cannot validly say that an animal is a vertebrate. On the latter count, even if the adverbs "only" and "necessarily" are elided, the statements "a vertebrate is not an animal" and "an animal is not a vertebrate" are not logical contraries, let alone strictly contrary as Dumont says they are. There is hence no double relation of "identity and contrariety" at issue, and there is no logical scandal. When, therefore, Dumont proceeds to state that this double relation is "stricter" in the case of a true whole than in that of a more or less arbitrary totality (p. 103), his contention is invalid; and it also shows, incidentally, that he is not using the criterion of strictness in a logical sense. Nevertheless, these are the grounds on which he next asserts that any relation of part to whole introduces hierarchy, and that essentially hierarchy is encompassment of the contrary (p. 104).

VII

The notion of "encompassment" (*englobement*) is central to Dumont's theory, and is perhaps the most important term in his argument. The translation from French into English is attested by the texts; "encompassment" in the lecture on value (1982:224–25) is rendered as *englobement* in the volume of collected essays (1983:243–44). But we have to make sure, nonetheless, that we have adequately understood what is normally conveyed by the French word.

The verb *englober* is recorded from 1611 with the meaning "to place in a whole" (Dauzat 1964:344 s.v. globe). In Littré it is defined as: "to unite in a single whole; [e.g.] the Romans incorporated [*englobèrent*] Judaea into their empire." The first point to emerge, therefore, is that the concept of a "whole" (*tout*) is basic, as one would expect from the adjective *global,* that which applies altogether to a whole. There is already a difference, however, from the English "encompassment," which means: the action of surrounding or forming a circle about something, especially in order to protect or attack; to contain. These senses are connected with the meaning of "compass" as bounds or limits; this word in turn is derived from Lat. *com-* + *passus,* step or pace, from *pandere,* stretch, extend. Here the emphasis falls on the action of tracing a course or boundary around whatever is in question; this object is thereby contained, but it does not follow that it constitutes a whole. It is this last notion, therefore, that we have to keep in mind when trying to understand Dumont's thought in its original expression. Nevertheless, we have learned that it cannot be presumed that he will use words in their strict, standard, or received senses (cf. Delfendahl 1973:65), and much will depend on construing his usage in particular statements.

A fair example is provided by the assertion that "high" ideas will both contradict and include "low" ideas: "I call this peculiar relation 'encompassment'." An idea that grows in importance and status acquires the property of encompassing its contrary (1982:224–25). Thus, in India, purity encompasses power. In an example closer to us, to speak of "goods and services" shows relations between men (services) as being subordinated to relations to things (goods). In studying a Melanesian system of exchanges, however, it would come nearer the mark to "reverse the priority" and to speak of prestations and goods; "I mean prestations (relations between men) including things or encompassing their contrary, things" (p. 225).

Apparently, then, we are to take this as an example of a high idea both contradicting and including a low idea. Under the most earnest scrutiny, however, it is exceedingly perplexing. The scale of evaluation against which ideas are to be ranked as high or low is not provided, and it is not self-evident. Presumably they will have to be separately assessed in each instance, though by what criteria is obscure, except that presumably these must be absolute and not relative. The example of goods and services does not help, if only because it is glossed with the implicit principle that what is named first, in a pair of terms, is superior and that what is named second is inferior, so that the latter is subordinate to the former. An initial objection is that it is not demonstrated that this principle holds in European discourse. Admitted, there are cultures (Sumba is one) in which the order of names or qualities in a pair is significant, but there is no such clear principle in English. "Men and women" might seem to fit Dumont's assumption, but at the lifeboats "Women and children first" does not. The names of complementary goods—pen and ink, knife and fork, nut and bolt—do not fit either. It may be that a sociolinguistic survey could find hints or traces of the principle in question, at any rate for some pairs and in some situations, but it is not a rule that is recognized by speakers of English. There is no good reason therefore to accept, in the Melanesian example, that in speaking of prestations and goods (in that order) one is reversing a priority. Moreover, the precise bearing of this example, in connection with encompassment, is not evident.

Let us assume, in Dumont's favor, that there is an exhaustive division between prestations and goods. (As a matter of fact, this it not requisite, or even normal; prestations can consist of services alone, so that they are themselves goods.) Still, it does not follow that relations between men shall be high and that the goods they exchange shall be low, or, for that matter, that they shall be compared on the same scale of evaluation. Let us also assume, though, that there is a patent categorical difference between persons and things. (As a comparative issue, this is just not true, and certainly we cannot know in advance what the Melanesian categories, their extension, and their interrelationship will be.) This still does not justify the assumption that prestations include things in the sense required; that is, as a conceptual subsumption of things under prestations, and in such a manner as to constitute a whole. When Dumont writes, crucially, of prestations "encompassing their contrary, things" (1982:225), this phrase neither explains encompassment nor justifies the allusion to contrariety. Encompassment allegedly both contradicts and includes; but contrariety is not identical with contradiction, and here too Dumont is using logical terms in senses that are not logical (excluding, that is, the possibility that he has simply made a logical mistake). In any event, it is hard to see why things should be considered the "contrary" of prestations, or in what respects they could be classed as contrary. The epithet "contrary" cannot be employed to clear effect without a precise stipulation of the sense in which it is to be understood (see above, chap. 4, sec. II). Dumont does not explain what he means by this word, in the present example, and one is left to conjecture whether it is not perhaps used here because some such hint of contrariety (if not of contradiction) is called for by the very notion of encompassment.

A prominent example of hierarchic opposition, and hence of encompassment, relates to an ethical distinction and may therefore be more readily comprehensible. Dumont writes: "good must contain evil while still being its contrary" (1982:224). In other words, the gloss runs, "real perfection is not the absence of evil but its perfect subordination; a world without evil could not possibly be good." This is a combination of a particular ethical theory with a logical commonplace; it does not follow from the initial proposition that good must contain evil, and indeed there is no logical connection with it. As for the cogency of the proposition itself: we can agree that good is contrary to evil by definition, but the opening assertion is nonetheless obscure if not impenetrable. It reads as though evil were included within the extension of good, rather as the class vertebrate is included in that of animal, so that the attributes of the subordinate will be included among those of

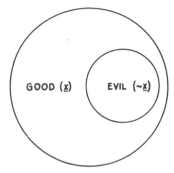

Figure 2. Encompassment: Good
and Evil (Dumont)

the superordinate. This can be displayed by means of a
Venn diagram, which is indeed ideally suited to illustrate
encompassment, as in figure 2.

But the attributes of evil are by definition incompatible
with those of good, so this would be a fallacious construction. Moreover, in the other example alluded to, vertebrate
is related to animal as species to genus; by the logic of division, species is subsumed under genus. But evil is not a
species of good, and it cannot be subsumed under good by
the method of genus and difference. There are also inconsistencies in the proposition, in any case. Encompassment
is said to combine identity and contrariety, or alternatively
inclusion and contradiction. But, in the present example of
good/evil, "contain" does not imply identity, so one of the
conditions of encompassment (or hierarchic opposition) is
lacking; and "contrary" is not the same as contradiction, so
the other condition too is lacking. Finally, the proposition
at issue is not the expression of what Dumont calls an ideology; it is composed by himself as an example for his own
expository purpose. He is therefore not responding to a
precept that is intrinsic to some tradition that exemplifies

encompassment, only in an idiocratic formulation, so this is not the reason for the logical defects and the inconsistencies of the assertion. The harder one scrutinizes it the more incomprehensible every aspect of it becomes—except for the evident force of Dumont's commitment to the notion of encompassment.

It will be obvious by this point that there is nothing in this notion to explain the opposition of right and left, and especially since Dumont himself declares that this relationship does not at first sight fall under the simple type of hierarchic opposition in which one term encompasses the other (1978:105). He does not explain, either, how it might be that at second sight the opposition might after all qualify as the required type of encompassment. We have in any case sufficiently considered the matter, with respect to the notions of whole and hierarchy, in section VI above. The topic does, however, lead us to consider Dumont's use of the term "level," which is inseparable from his conception of hierarchy.

VIII

In a society in which the right is preeminent, if something classed as of the left is accorded preeminence, this inversion indicates that "this level is clearly distinguished from the others in the indigenous ideology," and this fact in its turn calls for recognition as an important characteristic of the global ideology (1978:107). What does Dumont mean by "level" (*niveau*)?

The word *niveau* is not included in his lexicon (1983:264), a fact that presumably means that he does not consider it a technical or problematical term. It comes, anyway, from the Latin *libella,* a level (the instrument), which is derived from *libra,* a balance, or scales. This derivation is shared by the English "level," and in their standard senses the two words are practically equivalent, which in fact is how they are treated in the lecture on value and in its translation into French in the collected essays. This throws the stress the more firmly on the way that Dumont chooses to employ the idea of a level in his theory.

He uses it prominently, in fact, at the beginning of the first article, and at once one is put on the alert. He is describing certain tendencies in anthropology, which he distinguishes as (1) specialities, (2) more or less incompatible directions within the same field, and (3) private anthropologies tending to subject the discipline to nonanthropological preoccupations. He refers to these professional tendencies, not as divisions or varieties or fashions, but as "levels." The implication is that they are ranked in a hierarchy (properly speaking), the first at the top and the third at the bottom, and this scale of estimation is confirmed by Dumont's subsequent comments on them. There is no need to contest the discrimination of the tendencies or the relative estimations placed upon them: what is arresting here is the idiom of levels. The same idiom also characterizes Dumont's treatment of issues in theory and in ethnographic analysis, and he attaches special importance to it, for "non-moderns distinguish levels within a global view" whereas "moderns know only of substituting one special plane of consideration for another" (1982:211–12). Now the hierarchy of levels, it will be recalled (see above, sec. V), results from the very nature of the ideology, and it may be a universal feature such as would ground a universal concept in anthropological discourse (1978:101). The present question, then, is how convincing is the case that

Dumont makes for the concept of "level" when he comes to particular institutions.

The example that he describes as being so fine that one could not dream of a better (1978:106) is the reversal of orientation on passing over the threshold into a Kabyle house. He suggests that the interior space is qualitatively different from the exterior, that it is other and simultaneously the same (p. 107). This cannot be taken very seriously as analysis, but the sequel puts a different cast on the matter: "in passing over the threshold, we have passed from one level of life to another." What exactly does this mean? Nothing in the lines that follow this assertion does anything to explain or justify the allusion to a "level" of life. All that Dumont says on this score is that the distinction will "no doubt" be found in other forms in the culture, and that it is "probably" stronger in this instance than among people for whom such an inversion is not present. He certainly does not claim that the idea, or the image, of a level is intrinsic to Kabyle ideology, even though he states that in general the hierarchy of levels results from the very nature of ideology (p. 107). Equally certainly, there is no evidence that the metaphor of horizontal division corresponds to a particular conception of Kabyle space that for the people in question is represented by some other means, so that Dumont would be translating an exotic word into a familiar equivalent. And in any case the introduction of the word "level" contributes nothing to analysis. Instead, it diverts attention away from the analysis of certain social facts, and it obtrudes itself as a special semantic problem in the thought of the analyst, and this problem has to be resolved before the ethnographic evidence itself can be approached. What it is actually intended to mean could perhaps be guessed at, but that would hardly qualify as the analysis of an ideology. There is what appears to be a clue elsewhere, in a passage where Dumont praises Kluckhohn for being one of the rare anthropologists to have seen clearly the necessity to recognize "a hierarchy of levels" (1982:212); but all that Kluckhohn is quoted as saying is "different frames of reference" (n. 1), and this familiar phrase has none of the distinct strata-like properties of Dumont's peculiar idiom.

Although generalities about levels of experience abound in the texts under study, there are practically no detailed examples such as would help one to understand the idiom. On right and left, for instance, Dumont has, in this connection, only the following to say: "Rather than relating the level under consideration . . . to the upper level, that of the body, we [namely not Dumont himself but his errant colleagues] restrict our attention to one level at a time, we suppress subordination by pulling apart its elements" (1982:222). This phrase merely reiterates the burden of his contentions about hierarchy (which is confirmed by the reference to subordination), and it is open to the same criticisms as have already been advanced (see sec. VI). The present formulation implies that the body as a whole is at a superior level, and that the parts which are the hands or sides are at a subordinate level.

But this is a vacuous rephrasing, for the changed idiom, referring to levels instead of to part and whole, contributes nothing new to the "hierarchic" analysis. Actually, it impairs the argument, since part and whole are at least distinct notions, whereas in the present instance the solitary distinguishing epithet is "upper," carrying merely the implication that the other level in question is lower. In other words, not only is "level" undefined, but no criteria are specified by which one level can be distinguished from another. The idiom of levels is thus redundant to that of part and whole; it does not match the specificity of the latter vocabulary; and it contributes nothing to either the comprehension or the analysis of right/left as "perhaps the best example of a concrete relation indissolubly linked to human life through the senses" (1982:221).

IX

Finally, and closely implicated with the idiom of levels, there is the concept of reversal or inversion. We have seen enough of Dumont's theory by now to be fairly short with this topic.

It does not appear in Dumont's lexicon of key words (1983:264) under "inversion." The standard dictionary senses of this word in French are practically equivalent to those of "inversion" in English, as also of "reversal." It is again the use made of the notion by Dumont that must be the focus of particular interest. In the first article he introduces it in a general connection with opposition. A symmetric opposition, he writes, is reversible at will. But the inversion of an asymmetric opposition, on the contrary, is significant; the inverted opposition is not the same as the initial opposition. "If the inverted opposition is found in the same whole [*tout*] as that in which the direct opposition was present, this is evidence of a *change of level*" (1978:106). Here, he continues, the unity between the levels, and their distinctiveness, are both economically indicated: we are dealing with a whole, no longer just with a totality (*ensemble*), and it is highly probable that "one level is contained in the other (encompassment of the contrary, hierarchy in the strict sense)." These phrases have a familiar ring, but if we are to make anything precise of them we need to see how well they apply to particular cases.

We have already met reversal, if only glancingly, in the example of Kabyle space and the house; in the supposed symmetry between external and internal space, the latter is "reversed" in relation to the former. But Dumont immediately urges that we go beyond "this physical image" (1978:107), and he turns instead to other considerations such as quality and level. He taxes the editor of *Right & Left* with not pursuing the theme of reversal, in connection with the Nyoro princesses and diviners (1973:306–9), and with not systematizing it in this case; but he himself does not indicate what more ought to have been done in the analysis in question. Generalities and disparagements have preponderated, but there is no suggestion of an original analysis, let alone a justification of the postulated relation between reversal and levels in the analysis of opposition.

In the lecture on value, Dumont returns to the topic of reversal, as we have seen in section II above. The example he gives is that of the relationship between priest and king: in matters of religion the priest is superior, but in matters of public order the king is superior. In the outcome to this very brief illustration, however, Dumont does not in fact write of reversal. Instead he concludes: "This chiasmus is characteristic of hierarchy of the articulate type" (1982: 225). The situation he appears to have in view can be represented as in figure 3. Something of this kind must be figured, or else the *chi* (Gk. *X*) that is formed by the intersecting lines will not appear. That a merely grammatical chiasmus, in which the second phrase is an inversion of the first, is not what is in question is made sure by the connection with levels; here, religion is in some sense (Dumont asserts that it is a "logical relationship") "absolutely" supe-

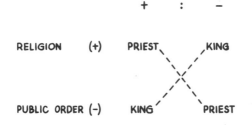

Figure 3. Chiasmus of Sovereignty

rior, while matters of public order are "subordinate." Not
that it is necessary, of course, let alone logically necessary,
that the relationship of priest and king shall be conceived as
in the figure. For certain analysts, especially those who
concentrate on systems of relations, an abstract conception
of this situation will be more normal and possibly more
desirable as a point of method. But the present issue is to
try to work out how Dumont sees it, and why he chooses
the words he does. Now the kind of "reversal" that he
presents as example is entirely familiar (there is in fact a
quite detailed treatment in *Right & Left*: xxvi–vii), but the
conceptual apparatus by means of which Dumont presents
it is not. It is possible that he has in mind a purely abstract
conception of the situation, despite the substantive cast of
his idiom, but, after what we have seen in the foregoing
scrutiny of his arguments, that does not seem very likely.
The balance of probability, therefore, is that the graphic
chiasmus in figure 3 is in a direct correspondence with
Dumont's intention. Certain interesting conclusions then
follow.

First, Dumont adds nothing to our general comprehension of this form of reversal; actually he says nothing at all
about it, except (what is either obscure or disputable) that
it is characteristic of hierarchy of the articulate type—a

type, moreover, that has not been defined. Second, the graphic chiasmus, with its levels (superior above, subordinate below), is produced within the kind of binary scheme that elsewhere Dumont so much rebukes in the work of his colleagues. Third, although he introduces the example as a reversal, he does not explain thereafter wherein it is a reversal, other than (implicitly) as a graphic artefact of dyads and levels. Fourth, although Dumont makes it a point of special criticism that the operation of reversal ought to be systematized, he gives no sign of appreciating that this is a very intricate matter. A systematic analysis of the concept (Needham 1983, chap. 5: "Reversals") shows in fact that a number of distinct and irreducible relations and modes have to be distinguished, and that "the notion of reversal does not denote a simple relation with a strict formal definition" (p. 117).

X

We embarked on a scrutiny of Dumont's theory because it made fundamental claims about opposition, dual symbolic classification, and techniques of analysis. He proposed a peculiar form of complementarity, and he laid special stress on the relations of part and whole, under the notion of encompassment. Also, he decried the work of his predecessors and colleagues, from Hertz (1909) onward, and he declared that in certain radical respects their approach was wholly mistaken.

A scrupulous assessment of his own views has failed, however, either to prove the cogency of his arguments or to bear out his charges against the arguments of other researchers. It has been found necessary to examine his assertions and examples at considerable length and in strict detail, in order in the first place to try to understand what exactly he was saying. This task was made unusually difficult by his use of familiar words in idiosyncratic senses, by the enlistment of logical terms for nonlogical ends, and by a demandingly abstruse manner of expression. The respect with which his contentions should ordinarily be received was subverted by a persistent misrepresentation of the analyses published by others, as well as by a haphazard and inconsistent exposition of his own case. In effect, what was taken for a challenging theory turned out to be rather specious and incoherent rhetoric.

These are regrettable conclusions, and they can properly give rise only to intellectual frustration and disappointment, but we cannot leave the matter there. What we still need to understand, if it is at all possible to do so, is what were the impulsions under which Dumont wrote as he did. We have speculated, after all, about the motivation of Steinberg, and we have also suggested factors that may have influenced Aristotle and Ogden in their writings about opposition. These cumulative indications give promise, indeed, of being the most revelatory findings of the present investigation, and already there are intimations that as much may be looked for from a sympathetic consideration of Dumont's frame of mind as well.

The first clue is the degree of fervor (all those italics, to begin with) that marks his argument, and especially perhaps those parts that are hardest to make out. This is evidently connected in part with certain commitments declared by Dumont himself. These are in the cause of the nonmodern, the integrated, and the variously articulated within a social whole; he desires, and in fact he thinks we need, a "highly complex hierarchical articulation" in a society such that "the distinction of levels should be present in the consciousness of the citizens" (1982:218 and n. 4). He is clearly against egalitarianism and individualism, as social ideals, and he is for hierarchy and totality. What kind of political system would satisfy these requirements is not our present concern, if only because the values that Dumont favors are quite likely to be of a temperamental kind that is not completely under the control of rational responsibility (cf. Needham 1985:10–11). The point of consequence here, from a methodological standpoint, is that these inclinations are in accord with the analytical model for which he argues. One can thus begin to understand the emphasis on encompassment, levels, and so on. But there is an important aspect of the model that is not accounted for by personal commitments.

Again and again in our critique of Dumont's theory, it has been striking to discern the reificatory cast of his thought and, even more critically, the spatial character of his expository idiom. The manner in which he presents his argument becomes far more apprehensible, though not more cogent, if we imagine his concepts as concrete entities, standing one above another, stacked in levels, fitting into one another, being turned round or transposed, and so on. It is very likely that the reification is, in part at any rate, or by reflection, the cause that he so misinterprets what he calls "binary classification" (that is, the method he imputes to certain anthropologists) as represented in a table of two columns, and that he ascribes to its practitioners the assumption that an ideology is all of a piece, "monolithic" (1978:103). The same tendency may be at work, as we have already glimpsed, in the way he writes about the chiasmus of priest and king. Seen under this aspect, also, it is telling that he should write that in modern ideology the previous hierarchical universe has fanned out into a collection of "flat" views (1982:222).

Naturally enough, not everything in the form of Dumont's theory is clarified by these factors. On a purely analytical count, is is certainly decisive that he should conceive classification exclusively as hierarchical and monothetic, to the disregard of the analogical and polythetic mode that is characteristic of symbolic systems (Needham 1980, chap. 2; 1983, chap. 3). But, all the same, it remains impressive that his contentions should so consistently be molded by nontheoretical and perhaps subliminal factors. Foremost among these is his impulsion to cast problems in the analysis of opposition, which is a spatial metaphor, in terms that are themselves extensively spatial.

Eight

Levels

Bring candid Eyes unto the perusal of men's works,
and let not Zoilism or
Detraction blast well-intended labours.

Sir Thomas Browne

I

At the end of his criticism of *Right & Left,* Dumont appends a long footnote in which he alludes, in a quite different tone, to an unpublished paper by Serge Tcherkézoff, a student at Paris, on binary classifications in east Africa. Not only is hierarchy "not absent" from this paper, we are told, but its author insists on the impossibility of reducing an ideology to a "dichotomous catalogue" and on the necessity instead to distinguish subsystems, concomitantly with the variety of contexts and the conceptual distinctions accompanying them, and to take into account the "syntactic logic" according to which these subsystems are arranged. Dumont is impelled to report this "convergence" with his own views in order principally to give due recognition to the merits of the independence and originality of expression shown by Tcherkézoff. "The spirit of the young Robert Hertz is therefore not dead" (1978: 108 n. 23).

Five years later there was published a monograph by Tcherkézoff, *Le Roi nyamwezi, la droite et la gauche* (The Nyamwezi King, Right and Left) (Tcherkézoff 1983). The subtitle identified it as a "comparative revision of dualist classifications." This work calls for some attention here, not in fact for the sake of any independence or originality but rather because it so sedulously emulates Dumont's views and idiom. Only whereas Dumont himself, in the two texts analyzed in the preceding chapter, provided hardly any material evidence or substantive examples, Tcherkézoff's monograph has the real merit of resorting throughout to abundant ethnographic data. Moreover, although the main part of the argument is devoted to Nyamwezi classifications, Tcherkézoff pays critical attention to Hertz, to three other essays in *Right & Left* (those on the Osage, China, and the Meru), and to other cases, in a critical and comparative perspective. Since his analyses are almost doctrinally faithful to Dumont's theory, venturing no development or revision, his work is especially valuable as a demonstration of the theory in a range of ethnographic cases to which it had not previously been applied. It will not be necessary, therefore, that we lay much stress on the formal cogency of the operative ideas, for they are those of Dumont and they have already been sufficiently scrutinized. Nor will it be feasible to reproduce all the details of the ethnographic contexts, but we shall concentrate on the extent to which Tcherkézoff's reliance on Dumont's idiom succeeds as effective analysis.

In order to do this it will at places be necessary to take

up disputed points from previous analyses. It cannot be presumed that these will be common knowledge, even among anthropologists, yet they cannot be reproduced here, so the ethnographic settings and other substantive matters will have to be taken largely for granted. Even the relatively minor extent to which ethnographic details are reproduced below will, it is to be feared, prove somewhat taxing (see above, chap. i, sec. III), but in this connection we may find salutary a passage from Aristotle (1961 : 366; cf. ix), as relayed by Pasicles of Rhodes: "Some demand strict accuracy in everything, while others are annoyed by it, either because they cannot follow the connection of thought or because they regard it as pettiness; for there is something about exactness which appears to some folk to be ungentlemanly . . . ." Our present attention, then, continues to focus with strict accuracy on opposition, as exhibited in the exact details of a system of dual symbolic classification, and it is this topic that will be continually at stake.

II

The introduction to Tcherkézoff's monograph signals his theoretical allegiances (Dumont, Lévi-Strauss) and registers certain analytical premises. A brief survey of the latter will help us, perhaps, to comprehend the main part of his argument.

After the initial inspiration of Hertz's study of the preeminence of the right hand (1909), he says, there have eventuated, particularly in examples taken from Africa, "binary right/left structures, hastily constructed in the form of two juxtaposed and partitioned paradigms" and characterized by "symmetry" (Tcherkézoff 1983:4). The particular examples are not named, but the implication is that the principles and the complexity recognized by Hertz have been departed from in the cause of simplification and reductionism. This outcome calls into question the validity of the approach responsible, which itself is problematic. It is what Tcherkézoff calls "the binary method," whereby "dualism becomes a simple logical complementarity that leaves no room for contradiction" (p. 5). This last point is stressed: all the accounts of traditional classifications reveal contradictions, but "modern logic" does not accept them as such. Thus the subtleties of traditional thought are viewed as differences of context and not as "a difference of levels of value within the unity of one and the same system of representations." But the coherence of that kind of thought can be recognized without being passed through the mill of our logical models; rather, it teaches us to see the particularity of our modern scientific thought (p. 6). So the binary method does not seem adequate to take account of classifications of the right/left type (p. 7). Indeed, Tcherkézoff promises to demonstrate, in the sequel, "the impossibility of constructing a binary table without gravely deforming the system." This deformation is the result of imposing on the symbols "a choice of binary arrangement (to the right *or* to the left)" (p. 6).

Evidently the debate is, as Tcherkézoff claims, fundamental; if a method of analysis deforms that which it is meant to explicate, something is very seriously amiss. The analysts in question are identified as the majority of the contributors to *Right & Left,* who are said to support the validity of the "binary method" (p. 5). But is there really any such distinct method? Certainly there are expository examples, and these can suggest questions and connections leading to what may be seen as a style of analysis, but this is very different from a method taken as a special and regulated procedure of a more or less technical kind. In this sense it is most contestable that there is any such method common to the analyses in *Right & Left,* and Tcherkézoff's characterization does not demonstrate anything of the kind.

Let us set aside, to begin with, the imputation that the binary tables (in two columns) are "hastily" constructed; this is too reminiscent of Dumont's allusion to simple oppositions "badly subsumed," and it is just as little to be taken seriously. Let us also set aside the description of such tables as consisting of two "paradigms"; neither column, as a sequence of homologous terms, constitutes a pattern or an example, and to call it a paradigm is just a misnomer. Also, whereas the columns are of course juxtaposed, it is not clear what Tcherkézoff has in mind when he says they are "partitioned" (*cloisonnés*), or partitioned off; this word already implies a whole that has been divided, but such a conception could not correctly be attributed to the analysts in question. It does, however, take us back to the opening words in the description of the tables. They are described as "binary right/left structures," but the only apposite word here is that they are binary. The terms "right" and "left" are included in the columns, but they do not define them; that is, there is not assumed to be any attribute of either term that is common to all the other terms in the same column. Nor do the two lists of terms compose a "structure"; they can be analyzed by reference to certain principles (duality, analogy, homology), but these do not necessarily consolidate the columns and their respective terms into a unitary structure. Finally, it is not correct that such tables (especially those in *Right & Left*) are taken to exhibit "symmetry." Tcherkézoff makes it clear that what he has in mind is some sort of symmetry within a dyad, for example "the opposition sacred/profane" (p. 4), though it is not at all clear what is symmetric about this. But what the tables actually sum up is the fact that each of the constituent dyads is asymmetric, in the sense that they are unequally valued in each of the definitive contexts.

In every single material respect except one (namely that the tables are, in some unspecified sense, binary) Tcherkézoff has thus given a mistaken account of the kind of table that he wishes to supersede. It should not be thought, incidentally, that the criticisms above take him too much to the letter. His aim is to invalidate a certain approach, and when he describes a typical product of that approach we must, if we are to take him seriously, take him to mean literally what he writes. By this standard he has evidently misunderstood, so far as the two-column table is concerned, what he describes as "the binary method."

But the tables themselves are not a method, and their construction is not in itself a method either. They are to be understood only in relation to the analyses on which they are based. Tcherkézoff ascribes to these analyses a method whereby "dualism becomes a simple logical complementarity." This too is mistaken, and on all three of the grounds invoked. Whether or not any of the individual dyads can be viewed as simple (correlatives are a conceivable example), a scheme of dual symbolic classification cannot be intrinsically simple; each of the dyads encapsulates the complexities of the contexts from which it is abstracted, and also the dyads are typically of different types one from another. The dyads are not isolated by logical criteria; the terms of each dyad do not necessarily or usually stand in a logical relationship (such as entailment or contradiction) to each other; and neither the presence nor the status of a dyad can be inferred from any other or from the set of dyads that represent the classification. Finally, complementarity has no intrinsic logical form; although the notion has been current in analyses, it has not been ascribed a logical character as a mode of valid inference. Nevertheless, Tcherkézoff goes on to say that the binary method leaves no room for contradiction. But this too is a mistaken formulation, for contradiction pertains to propositions, and typically the dyads in symbolic classification are not propositional.

Finally, he states that by the supposed method symbols are forced into a binary arrangement, "to the right *or* to the left." A number of misapprehensions are compressed into this phrase. To posit a binary ideology is not to claim that there is nothing else; a society need not employ only a single mode of classification. Accordingly, an analyst may claim to have determined a dual classification, but this is no obstacle to the recognition of triadic and other modes; in fact, it makes it easier to detect them. Then, there is no analytical sense in which symbols can be arranged to the right or to the left. This can be done when terms are entered in a two-column table, but not until the analysis of each dyad has been completed, and the eventual placement in the table is not a factor in the analysis. More fundamentally, the phrase seems to hark back to the implicit idea that all the terms in one column, either that in which "right" is included or that in which "left" is included, share a common attribute that is defined by right or by left, but this supposition is false.

The outcome, to this point, is that when Tcherkézoff asserts that it is impossible to construct a binary table without gravely deforming the system, he is under a number of misapprehensions. It is not easy to conjecture how he could so have mistaken the principles at work, and in practically every significant respect, for they are explicitly set out in the introduction to *Right & Left* (1973) and in the chapter on analogical classification in *Reconnaissances* (Needham 1980:41–62). Possibly the question has something to do with his decision not to take the time (in his own words) to summarize the long introduction, and with the fact that the latter work, although entered in his bibliography and tacked on to a footnote reference (p. 25, n. 3), is nowhere cited.

III

After his criticisms of what he represents as the binary method, Tcherkézoff registers his own position with regard to symmetry and hierarchy. It is in this part of his introduction that he enunciates the theoretical premises to the argument of his monograph. They relate to the opposition of right and left.

A distinction is drawn between "dualist" and "binary." The former refers to the simple statement of "the existence of two poles." The qualifier "binary" is the affirmation of a "logical condition": the relation is symmetric, or else asymmetric and in this case complementary, but still remaining on the same plane (*plan*). It can even happen sometimes that certain works do not raise the question of symmetry or of "nonsymmetry"; right and left are there only in order to name distinctions. In such analyses the symbolism of the society takes the form of a dichotomous table in which two columns link the pairs of contrasts; and "this appears symptomatic of an accentuation of the equal-status (*équistatuaire*) aspect, whatever may be the value—real or purely methodological—that the author means to accord to this mode of exposition" (pp. 8–9). If, on the contrary, the asymmetry of the relation is posited, the difference of value between the poles is underlined (p. 9).

Let us quickly comment on these points before proceeding to more basic matters in Tcherkézoff's methodology. There is no reason that he should not draw the distinction he does between "dualist" and "binary," but it would be more persuasive if a reason were given that they ought to be distinguished. Such a reason might consist in a demonstration that certain analyses of right/left did no more than simply state the existence of two poles, and then in an argument that this procedure is mistaken (or else, perhaps, correct yet insufficient), but neither ground of proof is supplied. Lacking actual examples of this approach and its consequences, we can only note the possibility and pass on to "binary."

This characterization is said to pertain to a logical condition, the relation being defined as symmetric or as asymmetric. But it is at least unconventional to describe the relation within a dyad of terms, for instance right/left, as logical. The contrast between symmetry and asymmetry has indeed a use in traditional logic—but only in reference to propositions. A symmetric proposition is one that is the same as its converse; e.g., the President is as powerful as Congress. This is a statement, moreover, that can be judged true or false, as can its converse. On the other hand, an asymmetric relation is incompatible with its converse; e.g., the President is subordinate to Congress. Here the relation is that of being subordinate to. . . . If this statement is true, its converse—namely, that Congress is subordinate to the President—must be false, and vice versa. But these are not conditions that attach to the contrast of terms in a dyad such as right/left, and it is a mistake to describe this relationship between terms as logical.

Unfortunately there is also another mistake of logic in Tcherkézoff's exposition. He states that certain works do not even raise the question of "symmetry or nonsymmetry," clearly intending that "nonsymmetry" shall correspond to "asymmetry" in the previous sentence. But in logic these are different concepts. A nonsymmetric relation is one that is sometimes symmetric and sometimes not; e.g., the President collaborates with Congress. Here the converse—that Congress collaborates with the President—may be true or it may not be true. It may be noted that the concept of nonsymmetry also attaches to propositions, so that the dyad right/left cannot logically be nonsymmetric any more than it can be logically asymmetric. Of course, there are other senses of "symmetry" and "asymmetry" that are not logical and that can be given an application in the study of dual classification; but Tcherkézoff expressly writes of a "logical condition," in connection with a "binary" relation, and in this respect what he writes is, by logical criteria, doubly fallacious.

The subsequent suggestion, that a table with two columns expresses a presumption that they are of equal status, is familiar, and it calls at this point for no more than the direct refutation already made in chapter 7. Those who have employed such tables, particularly in *Right & Left,* have made no such presumption but have instead argued explicitly for the converse, namely that the terms in each of the columns are of unequal status with respect to those in the other column. It is in any case a surprising supposition on Tcherkézoff's part that to list, for example, male/female and good/evil (table 1), or ethereal/terrestrial and flower/weed (table 2), or easy/difficult and normal/abnormal (table 5) in two columns should be thought to imply equality, either between the terms of a dyad or between dyads.

But Tcherkézoff goes on to add a curious qualification that attracts special attention. He insists that the form of the table is symptomatic of an equal-status view, and that this is so whatever the author intends by adopting this form. Specifically, whether an author ascribes to it a real character or alternatively a methodical utility, it betrays in itself a presumption that the terms in the columns are of equal status. By this view, nothing an author may say can refute the imputation. If he says, for instance, that the table is no more than a mnemonic device that simply lists the oppositions revealed by the analysis, and if the analysis argues consistently that the terms of each of the dyads are unequal, the table is actually symptomatic, Tcherkézoff proposes, of the view that they are equal.

The alternative approach that he presses for is to posit an asymmetric relationship; this underlines the difference of value between each of the poles (p. 9). If we do not "refuse to see the difference of planes (of *levels*)," the asymmetry appears as hierarchic. An opposition *a/b* in which *a* is superior expresses two facts: *a* is posited as a value, and *b* is subordinated as a contrary (*b* is "encompassed"). Tautologies aside, this is the vocabulary of Dumont, and the only point in recording the emulation at this point is to establish as much. Likewise with the statement that inversion, "far from being a contradiction," becomes operational and a signal of a "change of level" (p. 9). Also, Tcherkézoff shows by his examples that he subscribes to the view that a hierarchy can subsist between only two terms; thus, in the number symbolisms of the Nyamwezi and the Osage respectively, 2/3 and 7/6 are "hierarchies" (p. 10). All of these formulations are open to the criticisms brought to bear in chapter 7, which can be seen as invalidating them from the start, but let us all the same consider a real case against which they can be tested.

IV

The case chosen by Tcherkézoff, as the empirical part of his introductory critique of what he calls the binary method, is that of the left hand of the Mugwe, a religious personage among the Meru of Kenya. The major ethnographic source is the admirable and poignant monograph, *The Mugwe, A Failing Prophet* (1959), by Bernardo Bernardi.

An unusual aspect of the Mugwe is that he blesses with his left hand; it is described as sacred, and no one is allowed to see it, on pain of death. This special virtue attributed to the left was the subject of an analysis first published in 1960 (Needham 1960a) and later reprinted in *Right & Left* (1973, chap. 7); citations below will be from this volume. The framework within which an explanation was suggested was the establishment of a system of dual symbolic classification, such that "pairs of opposite terms are analogically related by the principle of complementary dualism" (p. 116). The central part of the analysis was schematized in a table in two columns headed respectively by right and left (p. 111), these being the terms from which the investigation had begun. It will be convenient to have the table reproduced here as table 7. The columns are transposed from their original dispositions (1960a : 25–26; cf. *Right & Left:* xxxv), but this makes no difference to the argument. No other alteration has been made here. The solidus in "woman / child," incidentally, does not stand for opposition but for and/or (p. 113). Overall, the analysis (hereafter referred to simply as such) appears to be a standard instance, perhaps even a paradigm (Tcherkézoff 1983 : 5), of what has been described as the binary method. Setting aside for the moment the objection that there is no such method, let us as far as possible entertain Tcherkézoff's premises and then attempt a detached consideration of his

TABLE 7
Scheme of Meru Symbolic Classification

right	left
north	south
Urio	Umotho
Igoki	Nkuene
white clans	black clans
day	night
first wife	co-wife
senior	junior
dominant age-division	subordinate age-division
man	woman/child
superior	inferior
east	west
sunrise	sunset
sun	—— (moon?)
light	darkness
sight (eyes)	(blindness)
——	black
elders	Mugwe
political power	religious authority
successors	predecessors
older	younger
white man	black man
cultivation	honey-collecting

case against the analysis. Some of his criticisms reflect his premises, others are variant interpretations of Bernardi's ethnography, and some others, unfortunately, have to do with textual discrepancies. The fairest approach, nevertheless, is not to lay special stress on one or another aspect of Tcherkézoff's argument but to take up its topics as he expounds them.

The beginning, as it happens, is rather misleading. "Eight oppositions," he writes, "lead to a general bipartition" (p. 15). The number of eight is an abbreviation of the twenty-one dyads in the table (not counting the two oppositions that are suggested but not confirmed), and the reduction is brought about by means of Tcherkézoff's summaries. There is no general bipartition, or in other words a division of a whole (the ideology) into two parts; what the analysis purports to have established is instead "a conceptual dichotomy operative in a number of contexts" (p. 119). That is, what is at issue is a principle, not a bipartition; this is expressed also in the comment that "the ascription of terms to one series in the scheme does not entail that they all share the particular attributes of any one term" (p. 117). The point was later reiterated as: "the dual scheme does not necessarily effect a total and exhaustive partition of all things and qualities into two mutually exclusive spheres" (*Right & Left*: xxvii). Tcherkézoff's reference to bipartition thus reflects a radical misunderstanding of the type of analysis at work, but also of something far more important. The analysis is intended to discern a mode of classification that is proper to Meru ideology, but to recast the abstract principle thereby isolated in the very different form of a concrete bipartition is to deform the ideology.

There is no need to recount Tcherkézoff's eight oppositions, for each of them summarizes a part of the analysis that he wishes to refute, and as he takes them up in order it will be convenient to follow him in doing so. But first he offers a general observation on the table: "On the plane of each opposition, the reference is sometimes obliterated in the concern to display complementarity; when the reference is adduced, it is sometimes located in the society, but without distinguishing the levels . . ." (pp. 16–17). We shall have to consider the justice of the first phrase as we proceed; as for the second, about the distinction of levels, this carries no weight since it begs the question. We are therefore free, without further ado, to examine the individual contentions.

V

The left hand of the Mugwe—of the Imenti subtribe—is used in blessing, and it holds the *kiragu,* insignia of his power; lifting it is enough to stop an enemy attacking his people. This belief is common to the Tharaka, Chuka, and Igembe subtribes also, but it is especially among the Imenti that the left hand of the Mugwe has become a source of great awe (Bernardi 1959:110). There is, however, another attribute of the Mugwe which Tcherkézoff selects as an opening test of the analysis. His treatment of this matter is quite revealing, and with this we can begin to adduce the ethnographic particulars. The point at issue, like others to follow in this chapter, cannot well be understood, and certainly cannot be decided, without resort to the crucial details reported in the ethnographic sources. These factual evidences may be found rather demanding, but they are essential: without them there can be no argument, let alone a theoretical experiment in the analysis of opposition.

Tcherkézoff remarks, quite correctly, that among the Tharaka the first Mugwe is said to have been born with a tail, like an animal (p. 17). As a matter of fact, "the tail is also considered the seat and the local source of his power" (Bernardi 1959:72); some elders still say the same of the living Mugwe. Tcherkézoff is less correct, however, when he says that this idea is also found "in numerous other parts of the country," for all the places and people that Bernardi names in this connection are still Tharaka (1959:63, 69,

73, 195). The Tharaka, incidentally, are not reckoned by Laughton as forming part of the Meru proper (1944:1). Moreover, Bernardi points out, "all the areas where I recorded this belief are marginal and relatively far from the residence of the Mugwe"; and at the place where the Mugwe lived his inquiries were met with a tolerant smile or with the retort, "Is he an animal to have a tail?" (p. 73). These particulars are significant, not just for the sake of factual accuracy, but because they show that, so far as the evidence goes, the idea that the Mugwe has his power in a tail is restricted to the Tharaka, and, among them, to marginal areas. So, whereas the Mugwe's power of blessing is thought to reside in his left hand among the Tharaka, the Chuka, and the Igembe subtribes, as well as among the Imenti, it is only in the backwoods of Tharaka that he is said to have, or to have had, a tail. This restricted distribution, as reported by Bernardi, has a limited bearing, consequently, on the analysis of Meru symbolic classification. There is, however, subsequent information that should at least be mentioned. Jurg Mahner, who later worked in Tigania, north of Imenti and northwest of Tharaka, reports that the Mwoko, original inhabitants who were conquered by the invading Meru, are said to have had tails. He also reports a current idea about "the clan of the Mugwe whose members are supposed to have tails" (Mahner 1971:407). This source is not mentioned by Tcherkézoff.

Nevertheless, Tcherkézoff interprets the matter more widely, in that he appears to think the idea about the Mugwe's tail is widespread in numerous parts of Meru country. He also makes a contrast between the Imenti, as partisans of the opposition of the hands, and the Tharaka, as holding a corresponding idea (*correspondant*) in the "opposition" of man with animal tail/"ordinary" men (p. 17), whereas in fact the Tharaka are also respecters of the Mugwe's left hand. The idea of the tail is held by them concomitantly with that of the left hand, and it does not conflict with the latter. Tcherkézoff's intention, though, in stressing the supposed opposition is to claim that it "can hardly be described in terms of complementarity." The critical point, apparently, is that right and left are represented by the analysis as being complementary, whereas a corresponding idea (about the tail) is not; therefore, the analysis is wrong in principle.

Actually, the premise is faulty; we do not know how right and left, mutually, are regarded by the Meru, and the analysis (p. 123) can offer no more than the inference that the right is generally preeminent. In the table, also, the left hand of the Mugwe is not entered, but only his religious authority in opposition to the political power of the elders. The comparison that is implied by Tcherkézoff has therefore no purchase. As for the tail of the Mugwe, the essential fact is that we know very little about it, and we have no evidence that it is conceived in some oppositive contrast with anything comparable. All we are told specifically is that the first Mugwe "was not like other men for in his body he has a tail like an animal" (Bernardi 1959:63; cf. 195), and that this tail has his "power" (p. 72). The reason, incidentally, that the tail is not considered in the analysis (nor therefore listed in the table) is not just that the idea is restricted and marginal, as well as being detached from that of the left hand; it is that there is simply no ethnographic evidence to analyze, so that we cannot tell where, if at all, it should fit into the structure of Meru symbolic classification. The "opposition" of man with animal tail/"ordinary" men that Tcherkézoff postulates is an arbitrary construction, and whether or not it can be described in terms of complementarity is not a real question; that is, it has no bearing on the comprehension of Meru ideology, and it is irrelevant to a critique of the analysis.

All the same, Tcherkézoff attempts to relate the issue to his methodological premises. This is crucial, and we have to try to understand him exactly. There is a gap, he says, one that is maximal, between man and animal. "More precisely, we find a complete change of level between the domain of man-animal marks and the level of the out-of-class being, neither man nor animal" (p. 17). A subsequent clarification is promised, but as they stand these contentions are hard to accept. The premise, to begin with, is quite factitious: there is no evidence that for the Meru there is a maximal gap, in this context, between man and animal; all we know is that the first Mugwe, in that he was born with a tail, was "not like" (all) other men. If by one account it is this tail that gives him the force by which he can do all his deeds (Bernardi 1959:72), still it does not follow that in this definitive respect he is assimilated to animals. We are not told that any animals possess this force, or that they possess it by having tails. In any case, the first Mugwe is not described as an animal; his appellation is rendered by Bernardi as "the man with a tail" (1959:72). This appendage is "a cause of great wonder and awe," but we are certainly not told that animals are regarded with either of these respectful emotions. Nor is the tail an ordinary tail, anyway, for "not everybody can see this wonderful thing with his own eyes." Tcherkézoff's premise is thus not only arbitrary, but so far as these particulars are concerned it seems very wide of the mark. His elaboration of the premise, so far as it can be conceded a discrete sense, can hardly be seen as more precise, and it leaves unexplained what is to be understood by "a complete change of level." All that is clear is that it does not respond to any ideological distinction reported in the Meru evidence.

As for the left hand of the Mugwe, all Tcherkézoff has to say is to wonder whether the "left" aspect of this personage is not also "an inversion *with change of level*" (p. 17). This is doubly obscure, for we are not told in what sense we are to conceive an inversion, or in what respects this operation is part of Meru symbolism, and we are not told what the levels implicated in this case are or for that matter what a "level" is. In the end, perhaps the most telling aspect of this opening part of the case, apart from the rectification of mistakes, is the extent of careful work on the ethnographic sources that is called for in response to a few assertions that were not formulated with as much care as they might have been.

VI

The next oppositions that Tcherkézoff singles out for inspection are north/south and right/left (p. 17). He admits that they can in fact be "superposed," as he puts it, in certain contexts, but he contends that in situations concerning the Mugwe the relation becomes complicated.

The points of argument are that *urio* means north and right, and that *umotho* means south and probably (analysis: 125–26 n. 9) left. The first complication alleged is that among the Imenti the Mugwe is not associated with the north-south division, which in any case has disappeared. There is no argumentative difficulty here, since it is not in fact proposed in the analysis that the Mugwe is associated with this territorial division. It is true that left, with which the Mugwe is connected, and south are in the same column in the table, but "associations within a series or set of homologous terms . . . have to be established by particulars and . . . they cannot be presumed by a general inference" (*Right & Left*: xxviii–ix). An association between the Mugwe of the Imenti and south is not established in the analysis, for the particular evidence required is not in Bernardi's ethnography. Fadiman, however, reports that in theory it actually was the Mugwe of South Imenti who originally "dispensed blessings to every section of Meru society," and that dispersal led to the emergence of "similar specialists of lesser stature" in Tigania and Igembe as well as in neighboring Tharaka and Chuka (Fadiman 1976:26; see also Fadiman 1973). What Tcherkézoff sees as further complication is that in other subtribes the territorial association of the Mugwe varies, but these variations are reported in detail in the analysis. Possibly he is making an improper inference from the table, and possibly also he has overlooked the lines explaining that this table "relates specifically to the Imenti, though the principle exhibited appears valid for at least some of the other sub-tribes" (p. 116).

With the significance of the colors black, white, and red we come to matters of more consequence. Tcherkézoff contends that, although they indicate a "ternary system," the analysis, as a study of oppositions, retains only the contrast white/black, white being taken as the superior, and that this procedure is the result of "the binary view" that is supposed to have occupied the author's mind from the start (p. 18). In one factual respect, a helpful correction is made. The analysis reports the ethnography as stating that there is really no difference between red clans and white clans (p. 112), but this is a mistake resulting from a confusion of *miiru,* black, with *mieru,* white (Bernardi 1959:9). The rectification is welcome, but Tcherkézoff then proceeds to discuss the colors, and the possibility that black might be superior, without reference to context. The particular point at issue concerns the clans of the Meru and the fact that the black and the red clans "formed a single group" (Bernardi 1959:9; see also Laughton 1944:2). Bernardi goes on to write: "this suggests a possible adjustment of the original names to a dual division" (p. 9), in other words that black and red clans would thus be contrasted with white clans. The analysis sums up the fact that "there was really no distinction" between certain clans by proposing the opposition white clans/black clans (p. 111; present table 7). This result can still stand, but the significance of red remains undetermined. In another context, "white men" are referred to as "red strangers" (Bernardi 1959:34), and in a myth of origin of all peoples, the first to be born was a black man and the second "a white man [lit. *umutune,* red]," and they started quarreling (pp. 193–94). So in these contexts red is equated with white, and in the latter place white (red) is opposed to black. The alternative associations of red, with black in one context and with white in others, suggests the possibility that it is an ambivalent or indeterminate symbol (cf. Jacobson-Widding 1979).

In this connection, there is an important addition to Meru ethnography in an article (not cited by Tcherkézoff) by Jurg Mahner (1975). In an extensive survey, he found that "men from white clans may marry girls from black or red clans, whereas men from black clans marry girls from white or red clans," and that men from red clans marry girls from white, black, and red clans in about the same proportions. In rituals, however, the red clans are said to join the black clans (p. 405). Also, Mahner relates, most of the clans with Mwoko (aboriginal) ancestors are black, whereas clans descended from "outsiders" are red or white. In the version he recorded of the myth of origin, or part of it, a man had two sons, one black and the other white: "the black was the firstborn and the white the second-born" (p. 407).

Finally, whether black and white carry constant values, in all contexts in which they are significant, is an open question. Tcherkézoff suggests that an argument for the superiority of white must be subject to caution (p. 18). This must be agreed, for caution is expressed in the analysis also; indeed, in the table "black" has not been provided with even a hypothetical opposite, and only in specific contexts (e.g., p. 115) is superiority invoked. For Tcherkézoff's part, however, it cannot be said that he has made an advance in the comprehension of Meru color symbolism; and it is noteworthy that nowhere, in treating this topic, does he adduce the notions of hierarchy and level. As for the ternary aspect, this is stressed in the analysis itself, with additional references to other places in Bernardi's ethnography at which "three seems to have a special significance" (p. 125 n. 8). If such a significance cannot be made out from the available evidence, this is not the fault of an analysis which proposes that "the triadic division presumably 'means' something" (n. 8).

The next opposition contested can be quickly treated. The analysis adduces evidence that men and women are differentially evaluated and that men are superior, in the contexts cited, to women (p. 113). The contexts refer to circumcision, political subjugation, and ritual. Tcherkézoff says that Bernardi's data are "too succinct," and he objects that it is difficult to put these facts "on the same plane" (p. 19). Whatever the allusion to a plane may mean, the objection seems to express a misapprehension. The point in bringing these evidences together is not to assert that the contexts are of the same type; they are patently very different. The point is to show that in various contexts women are depreciated in comparison with men, and the variety of the settings makes this point the more clearly.

The opposition sunrise/sunset also meets resistance. "The sun rises at the place of Mukuna-Ruku and sets at the place of the Mugwe" (Bernardi 1959:73). Tcherkézoff objects that this does not connect the Mugwe with the west, because Bernardi says (as the analysis in fact repeats) that the geographical connection cannot so easily be inferred. But Tcherkézoff does not give Bernardi's reason for hesitation. It is that a mythological interpretation affords, in his view, a better explanation: namely, "the sun, [like] the Mugwe, . . . cannot die, and therefore it sets at the place of the Mugwe" (p. 74). Where it sets is nonetheless in the west, and the "mythological" interpretation is not in conflict with this fact. Tcherkézoff passes on, however, to an elaboration that more decidedly misinterprets the analysis. He states that the west is purposely used in order to proceed to "the idea of darkness, which is, as everyone knows, devalued in relation to light" (p. 19). The phrase "as everyone knows" has no parallel in what the analysis actually says, and there is no suggestion there, either, that darkness is devalued. It seems that Tcherkézoff must have overlooked the long footnote in the analysis in which the Mugwe is likened in this connection to the Hindu god Varuṇa, who is associated with night (p. 127 n. 41) and who certainly cannot be regarded thereby as devalued (see *Right & Left*:xxvi–vii for a development of this comparison with Varuṇa; also Needham 1980:89–91 on the mystical and darkness). What is in fact suggested is that there may be an association with black, which is the color of the Mugwe's ritual staff, "permitting the inference that darkness is not symbolically incompatible with the Mugwe's ritual position" (p. 114). This cautious formulation is read by Tcherkézoff to very different effect: "The inferiority of the column of the left and of the Mugwe is found to be confirmed, at the price of two hypotheses that the ethnography does not support: Mugwe=west and darkness, and darkness=inferiority" (p. 19). This reading contains a number of flaws. The column in question is not said to be, as a whole, inferior; the opposition of the Mugwe to his counterparts, the elders, is one of "*complementarity . . .* rather than differential status" (p. 117). Nothing in the analysis claims therefore that the alleged inferiority is confirmed. The equation signs are in direct conflict with the explicit declaration that the association of terms in a column "rests on analogy" (p. 117), and they are posited in disregard of the accompanying examples that should have averted such equations of terms. Finally, darkness is nowhere devalued or described as inferior; instead it is glossed by a suggested association with black, a color reported as "sacred to God" (Bernardi 1959:92). It may be, of course, that the Meru saying "the sun . . . sets at the place of Mugwe" does not, for them, associate him with the darkness that directly follows the setting of the sun, even though the black clans are "those who came out during the night" (Bernardi 1959:194; cf. 58). Also, it may be that they do not associate the blackness of night with the black color of a sacrificial bull or the Mugwe's mantle or a ritual staff. But these are reasonable doubts (however tenuous) that Tcherkézoff does not contemplate.

The opposition successors/predecessors calls for no special attention; first, because in the analysis it is merely suggested as a possibility (p. 115) on which the evidence is not entirely consistent anyway (pp. 118, 126 n. 18); the subsequent evidence recorded by Mahner (see sec. VI above) tends, however, to support it, and the analysis is confirmed in that the white son dominates the black son (that is, the secondborn prevails over the firstborn). Secondly, Tcherkézoff misreports the analysis, and advances instead some speculations (p. 20), not worth relating, that have hardly any connection with the ethnography; the comparisons that he also adduces are not directly pertinent to the Meru case. The opposition cultivation/honey-collecting can similarly be passed over, since Tcherkézoff does scarcely more than repeat the ethnographic facts that are summed up in the analysis (p. 115), while proposing no alternative interpretation of them. In these instances also, it is worth mentioning, there is still nothing about levels.

VII

Finally, in the treatment of individual oppositions, we come to that of political power/religious authority. This is especially important both within the analysis and for its theoretical implications, and also for the weight that it is accorded in Tcherkézoff's critique.

The issue is summed up in the analysis as follows: "there was a distinct partition of sovereignty into the religious authority of the Mugwe, seen in his indispensable blessing, and the political power of the elders, seen in their effective jural and administrative control" (pp. 114–15). Tcherkézoff reports that this opposition has no basis, "in the very words of the author," except as a consequence of all the other dualities. There is surely some mistake here, for there are no such words in the analysis, and Tcherkézoff does not identify what he takes to be such. In any case, the fact is that the opposition is abstracted from a quite lengthy examination of the ethnographic evidence (p. 114), and this is what it is based on.

A second charge is that the entire analysis expresses a wish to see the Mugwe as only one of two poles, "and even that which is the less valued" (p. 20); the author of the analysis "*chooses* . . . to downgrade [*inférioriser*] the 'religious power' of the Mugwe" (p. 21). It is not easy to guess by what misreading Tcherkézoff arrives at this conclusion. The analysis reports that the elders look up to the Mugwe as their father, that he was their "chief," and that he is "the one person on whom the society could be said to focus" (p. 114); he is "higher" than the elders and "above" them (p. 117). But these encomia do not define the relationship either, and what the analysis stresses instead is the importance of context: "ritually, as a symbol of Meru unity, the Mugwe is superior to the elders, but politically he is definitely not." This formulation too is declared to be misleading, however, for "it is the *complementarity* . . . which should be emphasized, rather than differential status in opposed contexts" (p. 117).

If it is really very hard to see how these explicit reports and careful qualifications could have been construed as a deliberate assignment of the Mugwe to an inferior status, there is more perplexity yet when Tcherkézoff comes to explain why he rejects the principle of dual sovereignty itself, the opposition political power/religious authority. The prime reason he advances is that there is no ethnographic evidence for it. He refers to the duality of "powers" (already a significant misreading) as something that "nothing in the facts happens to suggest" (que rien dans les faits ne venait suggérer); "only the remark of Bernardi on the 'tribal government' that is in the hands of the elders serves to support the thesis" (p. 21). By this account of the matter, the partition of sovereignty is an almost complete fiction of the analyst; it is not even suggested by anything in the ethnography.

Let us test this contention by looking first at the evidence concerning the functions of the elders, and then at that concerning the Mugwe. Bernardi's reports will be related almost entirely verbatim, with no interpolations or glosses. The particulars that make up the next two paragraphs can be read therefore as standing effectively within quotation marks.

ELDERS

Traditional Meru society is composed of clans, and the elders of each clan control all of its corporate activity, ceremonial and political (Bernardi 1959: 12). The most important among the elders, the speakers, are the actual leaders of the clan in all matters (p. 13). Land is owned corporately by the clans (p. 11); all rights in land lie with the elders, and it is they who control its preservation and exploitation (Laughton 1944: 3, 5; cited in analysis: 115). Disputes are heard by the council of elders, who have power to pass judgment and to enforce it with fines and corporal punishment; a general council of all the elders of a place could pass sentence of death (Bernardi 1959: 13). Trying and discussing cases is the right and duty of the elders, who are formed into councils for the purpose; this is not part of the Mugwe's peculiar office (p. 123). There are also lineage elders, led by a speaker who convenes meetings of the elders and must always take part in all social transactions of the lineage; these include initiations and other ceremonies, marriage, trade, and cattle exchanges (pp. 14–15). In Meru society, authority in such matters as the above rests entirely with the elders (p. 22). The council of elders (*njuri,* a sort of general assembly) have so much strengthened their control of general matters that they have become the real masters of the country (p. 26). Laughton says of the *njuri,* as the legislative as well as the administrative body, "indeed it is the indigenous government" (1944:4). The elders control all forms of social and political activities; such control is exercised first in the inner councils of the elders of the clan, secondly in the larger assemblies of all the elders, and finally in the association and inner councils of the *njuri* (Bernardi 1959:150). Political matters are the subject of the assemblies or councils of elders (p. 139), and the elders in fact constitute the governing body (p. 153). Legislative and judicial activities are controlled by the councils of the elders (p. 154). Indeed, Bernardi concludes, the external machinery of tribal government and of social life would appear to work satisfactorily even without the Mugwe; that it does not do so, in the minds of the Meru, is confirmed by the unanimous opinion of all the elders that the country's general condition is satisfactory only if the authority of the Mugwe is efficient; things go wrong if the Mugwe is no longer respected and his authority disregarded (p. 155).

THE MUGWE

The Mugwe is a leading dignitary (p. 48), and his power is hereditary (p. 77). He is greater than an ordinary elder, and his power extends beyond the limits of a single clan; whatever he does is done for the whole of the country (p. 113), and he is regarded by all the elders with tremendous respect and fear (p. 39). He is the greatest and the best, compared with the present chiefs (p. 40); he has power, *unene* (p. 54), symbolized by the possession of *kiragu,* insignia of his office (p. 38); his power resides in it, and is derived from God's power (p. 62). The word *kiragu* appears to be derived from the verb *-raga,* to be hidden, and *-ragura,* to divine or uncover hidden things; no one is supposed to know about the *kiragu* except the Mugwe (p. 101). The Mugwe of the Imenti carries the *kiragu* in his left hand, and he keeps this hand concealed under his (black) mantle (p. 103). The power of the Mugwe is mainly described in terms of blessing; the Mugwe is there to bless (p. 137). The Mugwe of the Imenti blesses with the left hand (p. 74). It is enough for him to lift this hand in order to stop any enemy attacking his people; this belief is common among the Tharaka, the Chuka, the Igembe, and the Imenti subtribes (p. 110). The Mugwe blesses a new age-class and gives it a name; both functions are a privilege of the Mugwe (p. 24); he blesses the circumciser's knife (p. 111; cf. 193), and blessing the age-class is described as his primary duty (p. 137). He also blesses young initiates when they organize raids against neighboring tribes or subtribes, and these are not allowed without his blessing (p. 19; cf. 111); when the young men are away on a raid, the Mugwe is always thinking of them, and this is enough to ensure their victory (p. 109; cf. 119). Permission for the whole group of initiates to marry is formally given by a blessing of the Mugwe (p. 20). He blesses the poor; for instance, people who are in difficulties when collecting bridewealth (p. 116); and his blessing is also sought by pregnant or barren women (p. 118). His sanction is sought to confirm a sentence passed by the council of elders, even the *njuri;* if a man has been found guilty and has been condemned to die by the elders, he can find asylum at the house of the Mugwe, in which case the verdict of the Mugwe, whether favorable or not, is considered final (p. 119). The blessing of the Mugwe to close a dispute is regarded as a sanction and is highly respected (p. 119). Concomitantly, the Mugwe has the power to curse, especially with reference to the hatred of man for man and the abuse of sex (pp. 121–22). He can punish a thief by turning him into a wild beast; when restitution has been made, he will allow the thief to resume human form (p. 121; cf. above, sec. V). The consequence of disrespect and disobedience to the Mugwe is always described in terms of death, loss of one's children, destruction of one's family, or disaster for the whole country (p. 119). The Mugwe's relationship to God is very close, and he is even called God (p. 126); in all his prayers he addresses himself to God, never to the spirits of the ancestors (p. 127). When he blesses, his blessing and his interests are extended over the whole of his people; this universal character of the power and interests of the Mugwe is certainly a distinguishing mark of his office (p. 137). His presence is taken as a permanent guarantee of the continuity and prosperity of the country (p. 138); his insignia, especially the *kiragu* and the sacred honey, are considered to be the tribal symbols (p. 143). The religious and moral character of the Mugwe's authority is reflected in the attitude of the elders and of all the people towards him (p. 137). The unique quality of the Mugwe's power is emphasized by its religious character (p. 159). The office of the Mugwe is quite distinct from the inner organization that makes up the machinery of tribal government (p. 160). The authority of the Mugwe is, therefore, basically religious; he does not reign or govern (p. 161).

There are two matters in which this clear partition of sovereign functions might seem to lapse and to permit an overlap between elders and Mugwe. The elders perform sacrifices at deaths and in order to call down rain on the fields; but these occasions (certainly in the case of the former, probably in the latter) are the concern of the clan elders and are for the benefit of the clan (p. 13). The other matter is that the Mugwe is himself an elder (p. 151), first in his own clan and then at higher levels in the councils of elders; nevertheless, Bernardi speaks repeatedly (as at p. 150) of "the relationship of the Mugwe to the elders," and he also states that "the distinction between the Mugwe as a public man in high office and the Mugwe as a private man is consistently made by the elders" (p. 188). Thus the Mugwe assumes two different positions with regard to the elders: "one, which is official, as the Mugwe; the other, which is private, as an elder among elders" (p. 151). That the Mugwe's authority can be given a political extension (p. 139), and is a source of political power that a strong and ambitious man could exploit (p. 161; cf. analysis: 126 n. 17) is a contingent matter of fact, not a contradiction to the ideology. It resembles the fact that shrewd men, though not of the ruling age-class, could always prevail and practically run the country, whatever the age-class in power (p. 23 n. 1). Likewise, there are social issues in which the Mugwe is assisted by the elders, or which he discusses with them (p. 154), but this mutual implication in practical affairs does not affect the symbolic and functional contrasts between them. These can be epitomized by that between the elders as "the real masters of the country" (p. 150) and the Mugwe as "the symbol of tribal unity" (p. 153) whose "essential work" is to "bless the country as a whole" (p. 160).

This paradigmatic example of dual sovereignty is later explicitly recognized by Bernardi in another place, where he writes that "political power" belongs with the elders and that "religious power" is attributed to the Mugwe through the blessing and protection of the people, but that this must be exercised in "harmony" with the elders (Bernardi 1971 : 429). Also, the character of the Mugwe, as an institution, is "essentially religious"; his function is "integrated with the essentially political function of the elders" (p. 440; cited in *Right & Left*: xxxix n. 61). Bernardi remarks parenthetically that this integration emerges very well from the analysis presently at issue. He also reports an oral communication from Mahner, who carried out research among the Meru in 1969–71, to the effect that his findings "clearly confirmed the structural analysis" advanced in that analysis (p. 432; quoted in *Right & Left*: xxxii). Mahner himself later published his opinion that in Tigania "ritual authority and political power certainly were [as proposed in the analysis] vested in different persons and groups: viz. the *Mugwe* (a ritual leader) and the elders" (Mahner 1975 : 400). Fadiman, who also did research among the Meru, in 1969–70, does not comment on this relationship, but he does gloss the title of the Mugwe as "dispenser of blessings" (1976 : 26).

It should not be taken as unduly censorious to remark that none of these authorities, not even those quoted or cited in *Right & Left,* is mentioned by Tcherkézoff in his attempt to refute the hypothesis of dual sovereignty among the Meru. Independent validations of the analysis, on the part of ethnographers who have studied the Meru in the field (Mahner, significantly, some years after the publication of the analysis and with special attention to it) may not finally prove its correctness (see *Right & Left*: xxxii–iii); but they might well have been adduced in a charge (Tcherkézoff 1983:21) that the partition of sovereignty between the elders and the Mugwe is suggested by "nothing in the facts."

Another fact that may be thought consequential is that when Bernardi prepared an Italian version of his monograph on the Mugwe, he asked permission to include the analysis in it. He himself made the translation, and this forms appendix II in the new edition (Bernardi 1983:193–209; see 17–18).

VIII

Tcherkézoff concludes his treatment of the Meru case with the declaration that his "hypotheses" have one solitary object: "to oppose two principles in the investigation of symbolism" and thereby "to clarify the contradictions raised by the application of the binary method" (p. 25). We may conclude this chapter by considering some general features of his position.

The initial and continuing difficulty resides in what must be regarded as his imperfect comprehension of the work that he criticizes, combined with an unusual use of words. A prominent instance is his assertion that the two principles of a binary scheme are "reduced" to a complementarity of two powers which are reflected by the two hands (p. 4). "What is studied, in the end, is the opposition 'political power/religious authority'" (p. 5). The charge, therefore, is explicitly that of reductionism, and of reduction, moreover, to one opposition. A standard definition of reductionism is: the view that a system can be fully understood in terms of its isolated parts, or an idea in terms of simple concepts. If this is what Tcherkézoff has in mind, it is expressly refuted by the analysis itself as well as by subsequent commentaries. Of course, the postulate of dual sovereignty is important, and even central, since the problem is initially posed by the left hand of the Mugwe and its power to bless; this calls for a concentration on his mystical functions, and these entail a scrutiny of the secular government with which they are implicated. But the analysis attempts to understand the institution of the Mugwe "in terms of the structure, symbolic as well as social," that gives his office its proper significance; and "the most general notion by which this structure may be defined is that of complementary dualism, which appears to be a pervasive feature of traditional Meru culture" (p. 125). In other words, what is isolated is a "mode of classification" (p. 121) that is thought to be characteristic of this form of civilization. The point is certainly well grasped by Bernardi, the foremost ethnographer of the Meru, when he writes that the analysis "examines the entire system of cultural values of the Meru" (1971:431).

Moreover, it seems that Tcherkézoff must have failed to grasp the very principle of method that is carefully enunciated in the analysis itself. The association of terms listed in the scheme of dual classification (present table 7) "rests on analogy and is derived from a mode of categorization which orders the scheme, not from the possession of a specific property by means of which the character or presence of other terms may be deduced" (p. 117). There can hence be no question of reducing the significance of the classification to that of one of the constituent oppositions, such as political/religious or any other.

This is clear as a matter of explicit analytical principle. It is also unavoidable as a matter of practice, for one has only to try to reduce any of the oppositions to any of the others to see that it cannot be done. For instance, there are analogical connections between day/night and elders/Mugwe, but neither opposition can be reduced to the other. "Liaisons are made indirectly, by analogy, not by the positing of direct resemblance or equivalence or identity" (*Right & Left*: xxix). The passages just quoted mark essential apprehensions in the analysis of dual classification, but it is evident that the principle they express has not registered with Tcherkézoff when he asserts that the determination of dual sovereignty, in the analysis at issue, "was in fact a reduction" (p. 4). Admitted, it may be that when he uses this word he has in mind some sense other than the dictionary definitions cited above, so he may not mean what he appears to be saying; but, inasmuch as he provides no demonstration of an actual example of what he asserts to be a reduction, it is impossible to be sure.

This is indeed a recurrent kind of difficulty in what he writes. He speaks, for instance, of his "hypotheses," and there are admittedly such in the strict dictionary sense of suppositions made as a basis for reasoning, without the assumption that they are true; but if we look for elucidatory propositions, we seek in vain. What Tcherkézoff presents instead are reiterated assertions, and these are either untrue to the analysis or they are presumed not to stand in need of justification. Yet in fact it is frequently not possible even to be sure what he means. A prime example is his conception of something that he refers to as the binary method. If there is such a method, as a more or less technical and hence deliberate procedure of analysis, it must be capable of definition, but nowhere does Tcherkézoff set out what exactly he thinks it is. Similarly, he contends that "hierarchic analysis" is not only a "more rational tool" than is the binary method but that it also "permits the consideration of values" (p. 7); yet nowhere in his monograph does he define hierarchic analysis, any more than he explains in what precise respects it is more rational than anything else, or just how it better considers values than do those prior analyses (as in *Right & Left*) that actually consider values from the very start. In place of definition, argument, and analysis, he offers more or less abrupt assertions about "change of level" or "the totalizing level" (p. 10), and he declares that "only a structure of levels can account for this fact: that in a non-modern society to classify means to order the world according to a hierarchy of values" (p. 26).

Now the most frustrating of the deficiencies that characterize Tcherkézoff's exposition is that nowhere at all, from one end of the text to the other, does he think to define what the reader is to understand by the term "level." The nearest we come to a hint at a gloss is in a passage referring to the Osage. For them, the direction of the rising sun is sacred par excellence; "the sun represents a superior level" (p. 117). We are not told to whom it represents this (the essay by La Flesche [*Right & Left,* chap. 2] that is the source cited says nothing about levels), or in what analytical respect "superior" says more than "sacred" (though it surely says less). Nor is it feasible to work out some special meaning of the word "level" by a concerted examination of the uses to which it is put in Tcherkézoff's own analysis.

The main part of his book consists of a study of dual symbolic classification among the Nyamwezi (pp. 29–99). This is a system of much interest, but the extent of the ethnographic evidence prohibits an assessment of it here, or of the respects in which Tcherkézoff does or does not do it justice; that would call for at least a chapter far longer than this. What can be said, however, and in all fairness, is that his analysis is in essence entirely conventional. Despite his disclaimer about the provisional or experimental character of his procedure, all he does in effect is to isolate oppositions and to show the connections among them: left/right, man/woman, patrilateral/matrilateral, and so on. Apart from its idiom of hierarchy and levels, the exercise could in principle almost have been included in *Right & Left*. All that is distinctive (though not, as we have seen, singular) is the idiom and the train of contentious allusions to its superiority over the putative binary method. Even in the pages devoted specifically to the depiction of levels in the Nyamwezi classification (pp. 74–75), there is no explanation or argument to justify the term "level." Instead, there is only a diagrammatic distinction into a "superior level" and an "inferior level," cutting through all manner of persons, things, representations, and activities. This certainly is a "bipartition," with a vengeance.

In the absence of a critique, it would be going too far to assert here that the conflations and the divisions are nothing other than arbitrary, but it may certainly be said that as they stand the postulated levels are quite unrevealing. The reason for this vacuous outcome is that "level" stands for nothing in particular. Whenever the word is used, in relation to ethnographic data, it can be replaced with "context" or "setting" or "frame of reference." It would indeed have been advantageous to use these words, for it would then have been obvious that the contexts in question are not divided into just two types, "superior" and "inferior," but have to be appreciated (as in the Meru case) through their variety and in the light of abstract principles as well as intrinsic values. That Tcherkézoff does not do so is telling, and we shall return to the matter in a moment.

IX

In his concluding chapter, a methodological discursus on the comparative study of dual symbolism, Tcherkézoff enunciates certain precepts and statements of position. He sums up the aim of his enterprise as being to study "the antinomy between principle of symmetry and principle of asymmetry" (p. 129).

Now an antinomy is a conflict or contradiction between laws or propositions, and it is commonly taken as irresoluble; but there cannot be an antinomy between abstract relations such as symmetry or asymmetry. In any case, what Tcherkézoff calls symmetry is a characteristic fallaciously imputed to the thought of analysts who subscribe in fact, as we have seen (above, chap. 7, sec. VI), to no such premise. On a similar theme, he asks how it is possible to express a relation except by expressing its levels (p. 130); but the answer is that there are numerous ways of stating a relation and that none of them need make any mention of levels. He urges that "it should be conceived that inversion is not a contradiction; it is an *operation*" (p. 131), whereas it is not called a contradiction by those who have studied such matters (see Needham 1983, chap. 5: "Reversals") but is in fact conventionally treated as an operation (Needham 1979:39–41, 69; 1985:138)—only not, of course, one that involves levels.

As a final example of Tcherkézoff's way of going about things, there is his subscription (p. 133) of Durkheim and Mauss's premise that "classifications . . . are . . . systems of hierarchized notions" (cf. Durkheim and Mauss 1963:81)—"because," he adds, "they are referred to a whole." But what these authors actually say is that groups of things "stand in fixed relationships to each other and together form a single whole" (p. 81), not that they are hierarchized because they are referred to that whole; this is a formulation that is not to be found in their essay on primitive classification. Moreover, that seminal essay, first published in 1903, did not say the last word on the topic. Tcherkézoff's bibliography actually includes a work that argues, to the contrary, that "the logic of division into genus and species is not the sole pattern of all classification, and that things can be well ordered without recourse to a hierarchy of subordination" (Needham 1980:62). Instead, or in addition, there is to be recognized a distinct mode of nonhierarchical order, namely analogical classification. This argument, incidentally, takes as its paradigm case the scheme of Meru symbolism (pp. 49–57), but, as we have seen, Tcherkézoff does not cite it.

In sum, Tcherkézoff's argument suffers, it must be said, from a number of disabling inadequacies. It misrenders the analysis that it seeks to refute; imputes intentions that are neither declared nor implied; adduces evidence from one subtribe, the Tharaka (who may not belong to the Meru proper), in order to contest propositions about another, the Imenti (p. 25); ignores the assessments published by Bernardi and Mahner, ethnographers of the Meru, as to the cogency of the analysis; neglects crucial sources on the Meru; declines to spare the time (p. 25) to take into account publications on opposition and on analogical classification, put into print after 1960, even though these focus specifically on the Mugwe; uses purportedly logical terms (logical condition, contradiction, symmetry, asymmetry, antinomy) in nonlogical senses; and adduces ordinary words in idiosyncratic but undefined senses ("level"), or else in senses that are inconsonant with their ordinary meanings ("hierarchy" to connote no more than disparity or inequality). After this perturbing catalogue one may well be reminded of a critical phrase from Borges: "our surprise wavers between the arbitrariness of the method and the triviality of the conclusions" (1965:38). Only in this case there is no method, and there are no conclusions. There is indeed a recognizable rhetoric, but there are no corresponding hypotheses that could be entertained as distinct propositions of analysis or theory in relation to the full range of ethnographic evidence.

Naturally, in this case also we should like to know what factor of thought has been responsible for such an outcome. Sheer carelessness is not very interesting, and certain apparent motives are unmentionable, but there is one evident factor that once more is of much theoretical consequence. Here too, as in the preceding chapter, the overriding predisposition is a reificatory cast of mind. This is seen mainly in the insistent but uncritical resort to the metaphor of "level." This word is not employed as a metaphor, however, but substantively; it is applied as literally to an ideology as it might be to the horizontal material divisions of geological strata. It is thus presented as though it were a self-evident feature, and this apparent presumption is consistent with the otherwise inexplicable fact that "level" is nowhere defined. Similar considerations attach to the reliance on the notion of a whole (*tout*), as though this had a concrete extension, and to the conception of inversion as a quasi-material transposition of entities between planes of differing elevation. The predisposition at issue can be glimpsed also in another context that in itself invites no such approach; the oppositions north/south and right/left (above, sec. VI) are evidently related in Meru ideology (see analysis: 112), but for Tcherkézoff they are "superposed" (p. 17), as though one concrete entity were placed on top of another. The concept of opposition is not so prominent, under this aspect, as are the other figures of speech, but these in themselves are sufficient to make a case that applies to it also.

The shaping factor throughout is not only reificatory; concomitantly, it is also spatial, as is the idiom of levels and the rest. If it is true that a negative factor is also at work, as in the abstention from abstract concepts such as articulatory relations, this is subsidiary to the impulsion to cast collective representations as concrete forms and to frame the study of these, accordingly, in terms that are consistently spatial.

Nine

Grounds

To discover new mistakes.

G. C. *Lichtenberg*

I

The theory of hierarchy and levels, as formulated by Dumont and applied by Tcherkézoff, promised an advance in the analysis of opposition, first in connection with right/left and then more generally in the analysis of dual symbolic classification as a type of ideological system.

It is a disappointment that the theory proves to answer neither the questions raised by ethnography nor the questions that it raises about itself. Tcherkézoff's exploitation of the theory is doubly frustrating, for it creates needless distractions from the task of strict analysis yet provides no original interpretation of the social facts. An approach that claimed high theoretical value is sustained by little more than a simplistic idiom and a reification of metaphor; what is intended to show that previous work on opposition is wholly mistaken collapses into ineffectual rhetoric. This is really rather a pity, for the subject is serious and fundamental, and it calls for better treatment, but we can only respond to the arguments that the proponents of the theory have actually advanced. It is not up to us to conjecture a superior formulation of the ideas that inspire Dumont's theory, nor can it be our duty to apply them more effectively than Tcherkézoff has done. In the present outcome, at any rate, there is no coherent theory to be reformulated, and there is no rational method to be made more effective.

Nevertheless, not everything about these developments is negative, and there is in fact a positive interest to be found in the preoccupations of the theorists themselves. A chief value of the last two chapters is that they demonstrate the almost obsessive power of dualism and of spatial metaphor. On the former count, it is noteworthy that Dumont reduces the significance of hierarchy by defining it as a relation between only two terms, and that Tcherkézoff reduces the complexity of values in Nyamwezi ideology by representing them on only two levels. On the latter count, it has been abundantly demonstrated that the idiom of hierarchy and levels expresses a subservience to a spatial conception of opposition, its modes and operations. These conjoined preoccupations are not to be ascribed immediately to an incapacity for abstraction on the part of the theorists. A far more interesting possibility is that they evince, in theoretical formulations, certain proclivities of thought and imagination that are found in other thinkers and that may be characteristic of collective representations also.

This likelihood can be confirmed by the example of

Gregory Bateson, who certainly proved, in *Naven* (first ed., 1936), his capacity for abstraction but who showed a similar predilection for the spatial conception of dualism. In analyzing the ideology of the Iatmul of New Guinea, he arrived at the idea that there are two contrasting types of dualist thinking (1958:238). By dualism he means a tendency to see things, persons, or social groups as related together in pairs; and, according to the type of relationship that is seen between the elements of each pair, he speaks of dualism as being either "direct" or "diagonal."

In the case of direct dualism the relationship is seen as analogous to that which obtains (among the Iatmul) between a pair of siblings of the same sex, while in diagonal dualism the relationship is seen as analogous to that between a pair of men who have married each other's sisters. Direct dualism leads (as Bateson puts it) to concepts such as that of the Iatmul according to which everything in the world can be grouped in pairs, and such that in each pair one component is an elder sibling, while the other is a younger sibling of the same sex (p. 239). The diagonal way of thinking leads in Iatmul culture to the formation of artificial affinal relationships, and to the idea that everything in the world has its equal and opposite counterpart. Bateson suggests that it is possible that these two patterns of thought are both represented in the eidos of all cultures. After he had formulated the distinction in these terms, he realized that these concepts were only eidological analogues of complementary and symmetrical ethos, and that some simplification might have been introduced by substituting for "direct" the term "complementary," and for "diagonal" the term "symmetrical" (p. 237 n. 2).

We need not dwell on the justification for the distinction of the two types of dualism, or on the respective merits of

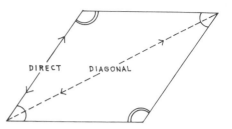

Figure 4. Types of Dualism
(Bateson)

the alternative designations for the types. What is of present interest is the original terminology and the means by which Bateson explained it: direct dualism would "classify together the adjacent corners of a rhombus (to employ a geometrical analogy)," whereas diagonal dualism would "classify together the diagonally opposite corners of a rhombus, stressing their fundamental equality and oppositeness" (pp. 238–39; see present fig. 4).

Now Bateson remarks only parenthetically that he is employing a geometric analogy, but what is really significant is that this conception is what he resorted to in the first place when he decided on (or found present to his mind) the epithets "direct" and "diagonal" as the designations for the two types of dualism. In other words, Bateson immediately thought of, and perhaps visualized, dualism in a spatial frame; and it was in spatial terms that he tried to persuade his readers of the contrast between the two modes of dual classification. There is no indication that in doing so he was responding to anything like a geometrical idiom in Iatmul ideology; in fact, the indigenous metaphor casts the two types of dualism in terms of descent and affinity. We do not know if there is a verbal concept in Iatmul corresponding to "opposite," but it does appear plain that they assort things by pairs. In employing (or explaining to an ethnographer) this mode of classification, they evidently call upon the notion of duality, for which they need only reckon so far as two, and on the two types of connexity that are exemplified for them by their system of descent and alliance. Korn's expert analysis of this system (1973, chap. 5) makes it easy to understand why the Iatmul metaphors for the types of pair that they distinguish should refer to descent and affinity; but at the same time the intricacy of the analysis, as well as the peculiarity of the system, makes it comprehensible that Bateson needed to translate the Iatmul representations into terms belonging to quite another sphere of experience. These terms, referring as they do to a geometric figure, are spatial in a paradigmatic sense, and this property makes the chief point to be taken in relation to the propensity that we have seen exhibited in the writings of Dumont and of Tcherkézoff.

In the case of Bateson, however, there is a curious aspect that goes further toward proving the strength of the impulsion in question. Granted that he resorted at once to a spatial representation of the abstract relation of dualism, still it is rather striking that he should have conceived the two modes within the frame of a rhombus. In the event, he found that those with whom he discussed the two types of dualism "tended to confuse the geometric oppositeness of diagonal dualism with the sort of oppositeness that occurs in the contrast between Day and Night" (1958:241 n. 1), a view that he was sure was a misconception. Despite the fact that he thinks it is "more difficult" for members of European society to think in terms of diagonal dualism, "because it is less developed in our eidos" (p. 239), it is significant that the geometric metaphor did not well serve the purpose of translation for which it had been adopted.

For that matter, it is not obvious, even in the present

perspective, why the adjacent corners and opposite corners of a rhombus should have been thought appropriate analogues of the two types of dualism. Bateson does not say as much, but presumably a reason is that he was thinking of the angles that are formed at the respective corners. The angles at adjacent corners add up to 180° but, whatever their individual values, they are always unequal: there are two of them, which constitutes the duality; they are adjacent, which means that the relationship is direct; and one is greater than the other, which can be taken to correspond to the different ages (at least) of elder and younger siblings of the same sex. By contrast, the angles at the opposite corners of a rhombus, whatever their individual values, are always the same: there are two of them; they are related on the diagonal; and each is the equal counterpart of the other, which could be taken to correspond to the feature of Iatmul ideology whereby persons so related (that is, like a pair of men who have married each other's sisters) are "nominally equal in status but always of the same sex" (p. 243).

We may or may not agree with Bateson that the phrasing of dualism as direct and diagonal is "in some respects clumsy" (p. 237 n. 2), but it can more easily be concluded that this particular spatial metaphor is neither lucid nor particularly appropriate, so it is not all that surprising to learn that others were confused by it or found it difficult. In order to make it explicit, as Bateson does not, we have had to try to infer what for him were the properties of a rhombus that made this geometric figure a suitable means for translating certain patterns or motifs (cf. p. 235) of Iatmul thought. This exercise provides a striking example, then, of a propensity to conceive relational abstractions in spatial terms.

But even this is not the end of the matter. When Bateson comes to revise his terminology, and to speak instead of complementary and symmetric dualism, he nevertheless remains subject to the same impulsion. The angles at adjacent corners of a rhombus may not be complementary in the strict sense of making up a sum of 90° (see above, chap. 6, sec. IV), but they are complementary in that, though each is variable and also different from the other, they make up a constant sum. It seems to be this geometric feature that Bateson has still in mind, if only because there is nothing patently complementary, in any formal sense, about the relationship between an older and a younger sibling—even if Bateson does say that difference in age is "the mark of complementary relationship" (p. 242 n. 2). As for symmetric dualism, here too the adjective is still taken from the field of spatial configurations, though it is not on a par with "complementary" in reference to a rhombus. In fact, taken strictly, it is inappropriate to this paradigm, for "symmetric" does not refer to opposite angles of equal value but to exact similarity of form about an axis of rotation; the symmetry of the rhombus is that the triangles into which it is diagonally divisible, each containing one of the angles in question, are identical as forms.

All the same, the geometric metaphor is maintained, despite the fact that the revised terminology introduces a discrepancy into the ethnographic exposition. When Bateson illustrates the idea of diagonal dualism, he says that this type of thought would "classify together" the diagonally opposite corners of a rhombus, stressing their fundamental equality and oppositeness (p. 239). But when he introduces the idea in connection with Iatmul society, he speaks instead of "the relationship" between a pair of men who have married each other's sisters (p. 238). Symmetry does not properly characterize the former case, which is the operation of classing together, but it does characterize (in a nongeometric sense) the latter case, which is a reciprocal relationship. Here, therefore, is a substantive lack of equivalence between the original terminology and the revision, despite the fact that the terms in each are similarly spatial.

In fact, the deeper we go into this instance of the employment of spatial metaphor, in the representation of dual or opposite abstractions, the more it appears as ill-fitted to the task. The analogy between the geometric figure and the motifs of Iatmul thought is inappropriate, and the revised terminology introduces discrepancies from the original and also within itself. These defects of analysis, together with the resultant impediments to the interpretation of Iatmul ideology, result from Bateson's insistence on introducing and sustaining a metaphor based on spatial properties.

This is not a singular failing on his part, as we have seen, but it is a typical accompaniment of anthropological thinking about dual classification and the relation of opposition. Now there seems to be no doubt that Iatmul ideology is dualistic, and that the Iatmul themselves distinguish two modes of dualism; but so far as the evidence goes they exemplify these dualisms by reference to social life (descent and alliance; moieties), not to geometric figures or to properties of space in general. (It could be that they associate descent and alliance respectively with contrasted territorial distributions of persons, but we do not know that they do.) Bateson's admirable monograph is thus of outstanding interest in this respect also: that it demonstrates, notwithstanding the acutely self-critical and detached style of analysis, the unconscious propensity of the analyst himself to represent abstractions by means of spatial metaphor.

This is a factor of thought that we have found in the western tradition back to Aristotle and the formation of the Greek language, and also in a range of other great civilizations of long antiquity. Related to this factor, however, is the mode of thought to which it responds, namely the apparently universal propensity to classify by pairs of "opposites." Let us now turn to the problem of accounting for the prevalence of dual classification as the institutionalized form of opposition.

II

Bateson's subtle and provocative work has brought us back to the grounds of opposition (as, in the present context, it has also brought us back to analysis), but his attempt to establish two basic types of dualism brings back to us, at the same time, the grounds on which typologies of opposites are to be resisted.

This resistance necessarily bears, in the first place, on the designations that are to be assigned to the terms composing what are isolated as dyads. We want to take nothing for granted, and we need to avoid the appearance of a theoretical commitment by virtue of the designations we employ; yet we have to use some words, and each of them can be seen as carrying a different implication (see above, chap. 3, sec. I). Leaving aside the technical distinctions of Aristotelian logic, we are presented with such general words as "antithesis" (Lloyd 1966:89), "contrasted couple" (Blanché 1966:15), or "pair" (Hallpike 1979:225), to which

can be added the word "dyad" that has been used throughout the present investigation. None of these words is exactly equivalent, in derivation or definition or usage, to
any of the others, let alone to the very word "opposition."
We need, therefore, to bear all of them in mind, whatever
the terminology of any particular phase of the argument,
just as we need to suspend the expectation that an eventual
formulation will accommodate them all or will express
some sense that they all share. One or another word may
seem to imply too much, whereas a word that conveys
merely the idea of duality may leave out the connexity that
we have been led to posit (above, chap. 6, sec. III). Moreover, even the premise that in any single instance there is a
relationship between only two terms, which may seem
uncontentious enough, can be called into doubt. Thus
Blanché, in distinguishing three "elementary systems" of
thought, lists contraries and contradictories, and then, following Coirault, what we have encountered as contraries
that admit intermediate terms—only he describes these last
not as dyads but as "triads comprising a mean between two
extremes" (1966:14; see above, chap. 4, sec. II).

According to this formulation, then, what we regard as
contraries, of this type, are dyadic only in consequence of
the fact that we tacitly elide the mediating term; this leaves,
by our own definitional decision, just the two extreme
terms, which are hence regarded as standing in a relationship of contrariety each to the other. It could perhaps be
said, in that case, that the mediating term instantiates the
relation, and this recourse might preserve the definition of
such contraries as dyadic. This is an artificial procedure,
however, and whether or not it was valid or advantageous
would depend on the criteria adopted and on the purpose

for which it was carried out. Alternatively, it could be contended that it is no more artificial than is the decision to define such a relation either as simply dyadic or else as triadic. The further we consider the matter, the more intricate it appears, and the more contingent the grounds of definition. But already the point of present relevance has been made, namely, that there is one mode of opposition that is not intrinsically or exclusively dyadic. If we continue to assume that duality is a fundamental property of our subject matter, so that our task is to determine relationships within dyads, it must be on condition that we recognize, in certain cases at least, that the duality is not a necessary component of the concept of opposition.

This qualification makes it all the clearer that "opposition" is not a single mode of relation. Thus we cannot adopt, for example, the convenient premise of Fischer (one of the authorities inspiring Ogden's monograph), in his treatise on the structure of thought, that it is primary. "We must begin," he writes, "by taking the prime form of relation quite abstractly; it is intended simply to denote an opposition, the members of which are each the condition of the other, and at the same time are resolved in a single datum" (Fischer 1931:68). Well, we cannot even assume that opposition is necessarily dyadic, let alone that it is primary or simple. As for the conditional aspects of the relation, by this supposedly axiomatic definition, and their purported resolution into a unity, these are features which, as we have seen (especially in chap. 6), are even more arbitrary as criteria of opposition. It is all the more essential, therefore, in the light of these lexical and prejudicial considerations, that we yet again resume our search for the grounds of this recalcitrant concept.

III

An excellent starting point to this venture is provided by Hallpike, in his radical and comprehensive work on the foundations of primitive thought (1979).

In his treatment of binary classification (pp. 224–35), he focuses on the contention that this is a fundamental property of human mental processes. He calls into question the view that all forms of binary classification—"such as alternation, opposition, and symmetry"—are logically reducible to a common form and are derived from a common origin. In fact, he writes, "it seems that psychologically the most basic binary classification is simple differentiation, which at the perceptual level takes the form of figure-ground discrimination and the awareness of discontinuity" (p. 224). However, he continues, differentiation does not of itself create a relationship between those things that are differentiated, for example, butter and tin tacks, but "relationships necessarily generate pairs because any relationship requires at least two elements" (p. 225).

There are a number of methods of generating pairs, and, in reviewing these, Hallpike is partly influenced by Ogden's work on opposition. The notions of break and reversibility accordingly find their place in this account, together with other factors of which as a group he states that "differentiation, relationship, boundary, break, axis, and reversibility of motion or variation are all mutually irreducible, and are all basic situations producing pairs, whether similar or dissimilar" (p. 226). He goes into interesting detail on complementaries, which he says are "inherently of part/whole type and are distinguished by a break [cf. Ogden's 'cut'] rather than by a boundary, and may be related logically or functionally" (p. 227). As examples of logical complementaries he cites debtor/creditor and husband/wife; we might alternatively call these correlatives, however, since their characteristic is that "either term implies the other"—and it is not obvious, moreover, wherein debtor and creditor form parts of a whole. Functional complementaries are such as lock/key, cartridge/gun, and, in some respects, male/female. These complementaries are dissimilar, but both logically and functionally one can have similar complementaries, for instance enemy/enemy and the dual divisions of Konso towns. Another kind of pair is that of "associates," whose elements are related by some kind of empirical conjunction, such as sun and moon or hammer and chisel; here the relationship is purely contingent and not derived from any logical or functional complementarity or scalar relationship. Correspondingly there are "dissociates," such as village/bush, which may be seen merely as different and not as contraries; sun and moon may be, "according to the classificatory system of the culture," either associates or dissociates.

Hallpike concludes his summary of the basic characteristics of pairs: "it is clear . . . that there is no one-one relationship" between differentiation, relation, boundary, and the rest, on the one hand, and contradictories, contraries, and so on, on the other (p. 227). There are, in brief, seven situations generating pairs, similar and dissimilar, and the pairs can be assorted by seven characteristics, but there is no systematic concordance between situations and characteristics (p. 228, table VIII).

These are commendably clear and useful considerations, with a decided outcome. Hallpike happens to mention opposition only incidentally, but his treatment of the various kinds of "pairs" comprehends nonetheless a typical range of what are commonly regarded as opposites. Of special

value is his demonstration that there is no effective correspondence between the means by which pairs are taken to
be produced and the types to which pairs can be assigned.
Expectably enough, in a compressed examination of a very
extensive topic, there are some points which cannot be accepted precisely as they stand, such as his reliance on the
criteria of break and reversibility, or his idea of what may
qualify as contradictories. But all in all this is a salutary account, more thorough and comprehensive as to fundamental principles of analysis than any other we have encountered. Now that we have acquired a summary acquaintance
with Hallpike's analysis, we are in a position to take up two
issues of major theoretical importance that he also raises.

IV

Hallpike readily concedes that there are mental processes
that generate pairs: these processes are differentiation and
comparison (p. 228) or alternatively the ability to distinguish together with the ability to perceive resemblance
(p. 225). "The only fundamental binary structures of the
mind, if they deserve that description, are differentiation
and comparison" (p. 235).

But these cognitive processes, necessary and therefore
fundamental as they are, do not suffice to account for
binary classification in its various modes. At three places in
his survey, Hallpike advances his own view of the reason
for "the prevalence of binary classification in primitive
thought, as in our own." First he states that this prevalence
"is due in considerable measure to the fact that 'pairs' of
various types are commonplace in the physical world"
(p. 225). Then, in more detail, he states that it is "clear that

the world itself is organized in such a way that pairs of various types are generated in great profusion"; so the prevalence of dualistic classification "is not principally a manifestation of a binary property of the human mind, imposing itself on a neutral range of phenomena, but rather an accommodation to a dualistic reality" (p. 228). Finally, after a passing allusion to "the twoness of reality" (p. 234), he states that binary classification "is not so much the result of the imposition of any 'binary structure' of the mind on to a neutral range of phenomena as [it is] an accommodation to the 'twoness' of reality" (p. 235).

The general drift of Hallpike's case seems plain enough: it is that both the organization of nature and some property of the mind contribute to the development of binary classifications. But it is not entirely clear from his various phrasings of the matter what relative weighting he gives to each of these factors. The prevalence of binary classification is due "in considerable measure" to the presence of natural pairs; it is "not principally" a manifestation of a mental tendency; it is "not so much" the result of mind as it is an accommodation to reality. In an introductory formulation of the issue, also, Hallpike writes that "binary classification in general is as much a reflection of certain structural features of the world as it is of the human mind" (p. 170). So the posited twoness of the physical world makes a considerable contribution to binary classification, or it makes a principal contribution, or else it makes an equal contribution.

From one point of view it could be maintained that the differences among these formulations are not very important, since the relative contributions of the two factors are not quantifiable, with the result that the issue is not empirically decidable. In that case, of course, one could wish that it had not been formulated, and in various phrasings, as though it were quantifiable and thus open to test by commensuration. Also, more fundamentally, it cannot be denied, without absurdity, that mental processes are at work, and it is reasonable to infer that the brain is responding to something outside itself. The alleged fact that pairs are commonplace in the physical world would be a fact registered by the brain (the "mental processes"), but we should have no means of comparing this apprehension with the physical phenomena that occasioned it. Moreover, that we registered the phenomena as pairs would not entail that "reality" was dual; and, conversely, if the external world were supposed to be organized in pairs, to some extent, this would not entail that our mental processes should register them as such, let alone go on to construct binary classifications.

These are general possibilities of objection to Hallpike's hypothesis, but it is important to note that they do not attach with like force to all hypotheses about propensities of the human mind. The idea that it is an intrinsic property of the brain to order representations by pairs is an inference from the comparative analysis of ethnographic evidences. Collective representations are indeed outside the individual brain that registers them, but they are not inaccessible. It is possible to discern in them (or to ascribe to them) various schemes of order, and very prominent among these is the kind of scheme usually referred to as dual classification. This provides a paradigm by which can be interpreted various other means of representation, apparently less systematic, such as polar expressions in English or the idiosyncratic imagery of a drawing by Steinberg. So whereas Hallpike's hypothesis poses an issue that, strictly speaking, is irresoluble, there is not the same difficulty in the way of

entertaining the idea that the prevalence of paired representations is a product of "a binary property of the human mind."

Notwithstanding the precautionary comments just
made, it remains feasible to assess Hallpike's hypothesis by
less demanding standards, and perhaps more in line with
what appear to be his premises. There remains at the same
time, however, a slight unclarity about what it is in the
world that is taken to present itself to the mind. The initial
reference is to "certain structural features of the world"
(p. 170), but the most detailed formulation in the expan-
sion that follows is that "the world itself is organized
in such a way that pairs of various types are generated"
(p. 228). It would appear, then, that what is structural is
the pair, and that the plurality of the features in question
consists of the various types of pairs. (We need not become
distracted, incidentally, by the linguistic fact that the word
"pair" can denote a set not limited to two, as of beads or
cards or steps, for Hallpike clearly has in mind the sense "a
set of two.") But what is not explained, by any reading, is
what particular phenomena of "the physical world" are to
be seen as actual examples of "a dualistic reality." This
makes a handicap to grasping what precisely Hallpike has
in mind when he alludes to the "great profusion" of pairs
testifying to the "twoness" of reality. Lacking examples
from this authority, we can turn instead to those suggested
by other writers, for the general idea (whatever the epistemological difficulties that attend it) is by no means new
or uncommon, as we shall see, and perhaps this is a reason
that Hallpike seems to take the pairs for granted.

Hertz, discussing the primitive division of the whole
universe into two spheres, the sacred and the profane,
writes that "all the oppositions presented by nature" ex-

hibit a fundamental dualism between the two contrary classes of supernatural powers, gods and demons. As examples, he cites: "light and dark, day and night, east and south in opposition to west and north." There is the same contrast, he continues, between "high and low, sky and earth" (1973:9).

This postulation of natural opposites is echoed by Lloyd in his study of polarity and analogy in early Greek thought (1966). In his introduction to the topic of polarity he remarks that a tendency to classify phenomena into opposite groups is found in a great many societies besides that of the ancient Greeks (p. 35), and he presents a survey of certain examples, beginning with the pioneering work done by Hertz. He isolates from the latter's essay a point that he regards as of great importance if we are to understand the significance that some pairs of opposites may have in primitive thought: "Certain manifest natural oppositions, such as day and night, male and female, and perhaps especially right and left, are often taken as the symbols or embodiments of fundamental religious or spiritual antitheses" (p. 38; see also Lloyd 1973:169). In this context he alludes also to "such concrete oppositions as right and left" as conveying what are, to our way of thinking, highly abstract concepts. In discussing a common tendency to correlate or identify the members of different pairs of opposites, he writes: "Often, of course, such correlations correspond to certain obvious facts of experience, as when day, light and white appear on one side of a Table of Opposites, and night, darkness and black on the other" (p. 40). Such correlations as the Greeks appear to have made between different pairs of opposites "reflect obvious empirical data"; the association of light and east and white, and sky and up, on the one hand, and of darkness and west and black, and earth and down, on the other, depends, in part at least, on "certain facts of experience" (pp. 46–47). And, in reference to Homer and Hesiod, he writes again explicitly of "natural oppositions" (p. 62). Here then we have clear statements of the idea that certain oppositions are natural: they are obvious, manifest in experience, and can be concrete.

These are arresting contentions, but they do not cohere into an integrated argument. Hallpike, however, advances two interpretations of the similar correspondence that he postulates: one is that the binary property (alternatively: binary structure) of the mind is an accommodation to pairs in the physical world; the other is that binary classification is a reflection of structural features of the world. He does not suggest what may be the causation of either of these operations, and to do so would probably be a speculative undertaking of a kind inconsonant with his empirical approach, but as they stand neither interpretation is immediately convincing. If there are natural pairs in our experience of the world, and if the mind is supposed to accommodate itself to them, it needs to be explained under what constraint or impulsion the mind tends to do so. It is not plausible that, for instance, such an adaptation would promote survival or secure an evolutionary advantage; binary classification is very unequally developed among peoples who have equally survived, and apparently with comparable satisfaction and security; there is no evident practical gain in a reliance on oppositions, and those civilizations that have made the greatest advances in science and technology have done so by transcending this mode of thought. If, on the other hand, binary classification reflects features of the physical world, it needs to be explained why it reflects dyadic features rather than others.

Hallpike proposes that there is a great profusion of pairs

in the organization of the world, but even on this premise there is no evident reason that the mind should reflect such pairs. Nature manifests many other profuse features, such as phenomena that constantly change and eventually die or terminate, yet the mind does not (or is not held to) systematically reflect these features simply by reason of their profusion. More fundamentally, there is no evident reason to accept that the organization of the physical world, or the prevalence of phenomena of a certain kind, should be imitated in the classification of other phenomena that do not exhibit that organization. It would be quite another matter if the hypothesis were that the mind, being predisposed to classify in binary terms, then responded to the alleged pairs in nature and adopted for its own ends the contrasts that they proffered. This would be a more plausible suggestion, but of course it is contradictory to the hypothesis of reflection, which is intended to explain away the propensity on which this alternative is premised.

Much the same arguments work against the implication of what Hertz and Lloyd say about natural oppositions, to the extent that they seem to make a tacit assumption that the natural to some extent determines the cultural. Lloyd is for the most part more prudent, however, in that he generally limits himself to the position that natural oppositions are taken as symbols or embodiments of mystical antitheses, or to the observation that there is a correspondence with certain facts of experience, even though he does also suggest that some Greek correlations "reflect" obvious empirical data. Nevertheless, even his more cautious formulations pertain to a quite definite commitment to the postulate that there are oppositions in nature, and it is this premise that calls for examination.

V

The case against natural oppositions can be succinctly stated by the adoption from another context of a phrase by Cassirer: "nature comes into being through a theoretical interpretation and elaboration of sensory contents" (1953–57, 2:193). This proposition can be borne out by an examination of the first of the natural oppositions common to the lists of Hertz and Lloyd, namely that of day/night.

Let us imagine a photometer set out in the open and in optimum conditions for the registration of natural light; for example, out on a plain and far removed from any sources of artificial light or their reflections from clouds. The conditions are meant to be primitive. The trace recorded by the instrument would be something like that which is schematically shown in figure 5. In this figure the upper horizontal (+) stands for a maximum intensity of light; this is an arbitrary limit, but we can imagine it as that of the naked sun. The lower horizontal (−) stands for a complete absence of light; this limit is not arbitrary, though it is virtual and not real. The photometer, recording the circumambient light such as would normally impinge on the human eye, will produce a trace showing a maximum intensity for some time during the day and a minimum for some time during the night. Over a succession of days the time of the maximum will vary from day to day, according to such factors as clouds or dust storms, and so also the time of the minimum will vary from night to night. These variations (not shown by a time scale on the figure, but easily conceived) constitute one form of irregularity. A more important feature is that the maximum intensity of light recorded on successive days will also vary; and so too will

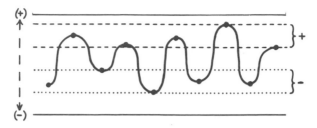

Figure 5. Diurnal Fluctuation of Light and Dark (Schematic)

the minimum intensity recorded on successive nights. The maxima of the trace will never, of course, reach the upper limit of intensity; there is no physical limit, and the arbitrary limit depicted is set above the intensity of any of the maxima. The minima of the trace will never reach the lower limit; whatever the atmospheric conditions, there will always be registered some degree of radiance from the stars, not to mention the moon. The points of maximum intensity will thus fall within a certain range, and the points of minimum intensity will fall within a lower range. The lowest point on the upper range, as recorded on an extremely overcast day or in a storm of dust or snow, can be close to (or can even coincide with, or fall below) the highest point in the lower range, registering for instance a clear sky and a full moon.

It is this irregular pattern of variations that provides the "sensory contents" of what are distinguished as "day" and "night." There is no steady duality dividing the phenomena into two and corresponding to the pair of lexical concepts. The binary discrimination day/night is composed of two abstractions from among ranges of irregular intensities of natural light, but there is no natural opposition corresponding to the lexical distinction. The neat dyad of day/

night is a "theoretical interpretation" of a perpetual but in-constant fluctuation produced by the irregular changes of a variety of physical phenomena. There is of course an extent of time within each twenty-four hours (in a temperate or tropical latitude, let us stipulate) in which the sun is in the sky, but this does not set natural limits to what is called "day," nor concomitantly does it set natural limits to what is called "night." Quite a long time before the sun (or part of it; one has to decide what is to count) is visible on or above the horizon there is "first light," and for a comparable time after the sun has set there is a period of twilight. In English there is then a distinction made between twilight and the deeper gloom of dusk. There is no clear line of natural contrast between day and night except by means of the arbitrary, and hence culturally variable, criteria of collective representations. What might be taken for a paradigmatic natural opposition is instead a cultural artefact.

The same is true of the "duality" that Lloyd ascribes to the course of the sun, which "rises in one quarter of the sky and sets in the opposite quarter" (1966:80). In this case, the sun actually traces a long arc across the sky for as long as it is visible; to call the initial and terminal points sunrise and sunset is to make a selection from among the points that compose the arc and to place an interpretation on them. To say that the sun rises and sets in "opposite" quarters either begs the question or is inexact; it is only when the sun passes directly overhead at its zenith that it rises and sets, from the point of view of the human observer on the ground, at opposite points, and even then these points have to be first singled out and then conjoined as opposites if a duality is to be constituted. Also, to say that "day alternates with night" (p. 80) is premised on duality; and although the concept of alternation may be an index to a common and spontaneous inclination of thought (Needham 1983:154), still it is a concept and not an autonomous fact of experience.

Another candidate for the role of natural opposition, mentioned as such by Lloyd, is male/female. This looks like an "obvious fact of experience," and possibly it is one of the pairs in nature that Hallpike has in mind as instances of "twoness in reality." Certainly there are marked differences of anatomy and in secondary sexual characteristics between male and female in many species, though they are not always obvious; to the untrained eye there may not seem much difference between male and female quails (especially as members of the same sex frequently trample one another), and the differences between male and female hyenas are so hard to detect that for a long time they were thought to be hermaphrodites. But let us take as a test case the opposition man/woman. This pertains to our own species, and is likely to be of the greatest social importance.

Genetically there is an absolute distinction between man and woman, but from a cultural point of view we can ignore chromosomes. In genitalia and body build there are also gross differences between the sexes, but they are by no means so clear-cut. The external organs can vary greatly, to the point of hermaphroditism; an anatomical male can have the contours of a woman, and an anatomical female can be built like a man; a man has nipples as though he were a woman, and a woman has a homologue to the penis as though she were a man. In these descriptions, however, we have already resorted tacitly to conceptions of man and woman which are not given as natural isolates but are cultural ideals. The physical reality is that there is an immense array of physical types, and that not even the visible genitalia mark off an absolute dividing line between men and women.

When we take social characteristics into account, the matter becomes far more complicated; not only do societies distinguish men from women by different criteria of dress and comportment, but they allow for combinations of physical and social characteristics that increase the number of sexes beyond two. Thus among the Nuer a woman can so far acquire the status of a man that she can marry a woman and be reckoned the father of the latter's children; conversely, among the Ngaju a shaman can assume all the signs of femininity, and among the Chukchee such a person can marry a man and claim to bear children. Admittedly, in these cases the transformations are effected by reference to an initial distinction of two sexes, but the outcome does not fall within that classification; the manly woman is not a man like other men, and the feminized man is not a woman like other women, but each is of a distinct kind characterized by a combination of anatomical and social criteria. If a sex is defined by both types of criteria, and if the man/woman paradigm is defined by criteria of like kinds, then the transformations in question create a total of four sexes. And if, as among the Chukchee, there are recognized degrees of manhood, and similar degrees of womanhood, then it can be envisaged that the number of the sexes will be more than four. Of course, these considerations are based on what we distinguish as a sex, and it seems that in non-Indo-European societies there is in general no such distinct lexical category, but this contrast does not undermine the comparison; instead, it adds to the evidence that a classification of human beings into two sexes is not a natural opposition.

Furthermore, when we include the criteria of psychological theories among the distinctive features of sexual identity, there are innumerable additional complications. By some criteria there are no differences between the anatomical sexes; by other psychological criteria each human being embodies a blend of masculine and feminine characteristics (assuming the criteria to be so divided in the first place, which is not a premise to be taken for granted), so that in place of two distinct sexes there is a scale of variation or even an unordered array of complex singularities. The more factors we admit into the comparison, therefore, the plainer it becomes that the conceptual pair man/woman is not a natural opposition.

VI

The dyad right/left, the third of Lloyd's manifest natural oppositions, is more difficult to deal with.

It is described as a concrete opposition, the idea presumably being not that the relation itself is concrete but that the hands, as emblems of the sides, are physical objects. Lloyd does not explicitly refer to the hands, though he does mention Hertz on handedness in the same paragraph, and then goes on to say that "the distinction between the two sides of the body, and their symmetry, are, of course, facts of experience" (1966:39). It could be said, for that matter, that at the place in question he conflates hands, sides, and directions, and indeed his argument applies to all three aspects of laterality. Only the hands and the sides, however, are concrete, and of these it is the hands that are the more readily isolable as distinct objects. Let us therefore take these first, as being the most favorable to the hypothesis that right and left make up a natural opposition. In this case, also, we are apparently meant to apprehend the phenomena naively, so far as that can be done, without resort to a prior lexical classification, for to call them "hands" already constitutes the pair that we take to be in question. Whether or not this is what is intended by our authors, the procedure certainly corresponds more nearly to the idea that the opposition is natural, or is presented by reality.

The hands (as at present we have to call them) are certainly more like each other than they are like other parts of the body such as the feet. They are alike in form, though they are nevertheless enantiomorphs. They are also alike in functions, even if there is an innate predisposition toward handedness. It can be conceded that they are more alike than they are unlike, even if the disparities are evident and considerable, and there are only two of them. Let us accept therefore that they appear to constitute what Hallpike calls a pair, and also that they may thereby provide the grounds for what Lloyd calls a natural opposition. We can easily add, moreover, that as members of the body they are more prominent than other parts; we also possess two feet, two ears, and two nostrils, yet these are not commonly singled out as pairs in the way that hands are. Even our two eyes, which are of such physical and social importance, are not usually adopted as emblems of opposition. Swedenborg did so (see Needham 1985 : 126), but this is an idiosyncratic idea and not widely to be found in collective representations. So we have gone quite a way toward recognizing the hands as a natural pair. But the apparent strength of the case makes it the more plainly vulnerable to the epistemological objection that this pair has nonetheless to be conceived as a pair, just as concomitantly it has to be evaluated as a specially significant pair. If, ex hypothesi, it is apprehended (as a quasi-pair) before the hands are named together by the same word, then there is some act of the mind that classes them together as two things of a kind; and when a significance is attributed to these things, over and above other parts of the body, evaluative factors are introduced which are distinct from the apprehension that they are two things. In this case in particular, therefore, it appears that the idea of a natural pair, let alone that of a natural opposition, cannot be proved correct.

There is a further difficulty with the idea that the distinction between the two sides of the body is a fact of experience. It is true that laterally enantiomorphic surfaces of the body (what we ordinarily call the right and left sides) can be sensorily contrasted, so that events in the one are not ascribed to the other; also this discrimination is probably part of the body image. But these phenomena are not homogeneous, or even isomorphic, with a "distinction" between two "sides." The distinction is a conceptual operation, and it cannot in itself be experienced. As an act of classification, moreover, it depends on the tracing of a vertical boundary, such as the median line postulated by the Temne, between what are thereby distinguished as the two sides. This line of division is certainly not a fact of experience. One does not, for instance, spontaneously sense a point that is a centimeter to the right of the navel as belonging to the right side. A pin-prick there will no doubt be ascribed to the right side, if this is reckoned from the navel, just as will a body-image location of that point, but this recognition depends on a prior classification that is not a fact of experience but is a cultural partition of what is physically an entity with a continuous surface. If the two sides are defined more vaguely (as in ordinary speech) and without reference to a median line, leaving in between an indeterminate region that is neither right nor left, then this different conception of the body emphasizes that it is indeed a conception that is at work and that such conceptions can vary. As for the lateral symmetry of the body, this too is a conceptual attribute and not a natural form within which the two sides present themselves. So it cannot be accepted that the sides of the body are instances of the "twoness of reality" or that they are even the grounds of a natural opposition.

There is a curious interest, incidentally, in the global distribution of a class of imaginary beings that are one-sided (Needham 1980, chap. 1: "Unilateral Figures"), for this kind of collective representation goes to show that, according to the apparent operation of a subliminal impulsion, the body is not necessarily constituted by two sides. A comparable tendency of the imagination is seen also artificially, in Italo Calvino's novel about a character who, vertically divided, lives two separate lives as two half-men (Calvino 1955)—even if Calvino does get the moral attributes of the sides the wrong way round. Of course, the image of a unilateral figure is premised on the prior ascription of two sides to the real body, but then it stresses the fact that this also is a collective representation and hence nonnatural, even if less obviously so than is the unnatural oddity of the half-man.

Finally there is the third construction that can be placed on Lloyd's proposal, namely that right and left as directions (with reference to the hands or the sides) make up a natural opposition. It would accord well with an earlier part of the present argument (chap. 3, sec. III) to think that there is a natural sense of right and left, but this hypothesis is even shakier than are those that we have just examined. The human body does not have flat sides to which right and left can be regarded as perpendicular; it is more or less round, at the trunk, and the flanks are indeterminate convex surfaces, so on neither side is there a straight base line to which the lateral direction would be at right angles (cf.

fig. 1). Instead, there is a quadrant on the right within which the direction "right" can be specified more or less accurately, and similarly there is a quadrant on the left. Let us imagine a vertical center line within the body, and stipulate that 0/360° is straight ahead. Ideally it might be taken that right would be at an angle of 90° and left on a bearing of 270°. But in the first place these bearings have to be stipulated as ideal, that is as the strict senses of right and left. A rank of soldiers should stand so, with reference to one another, and in dressing by the right they will form a straight line, but this is an artificial and quasi-ceremonial ordering, not one that could be thought at all natural. In ordinary discourse, "right" can easily be any direction within, say, 45° and 135°; if someone is advised that something he seeks is on his right, he may very well cast about within such a quadrant, and he will not give up if it proves not to be located at 90° from his imagined center line. This example introduces, furthermore, the fact that similar considerations obtain with reference both to one's own body and to the body of someone else. In neither case is right/left, as an opposition of lateral directions, given as a pair in the physical world; but in each case the directions are cultural definitions, and what precisely is to count as to the right or to the left depends on the linguistic conventions governing contingent circumstances.

VII

There are thus very considerable difficulties in the way of accepting the hypothesis that the world generates pairs or that there are obvious facts of experience constituting manifest natural oppositions.

Instead, in each case considered, the duality (not to mention the enigmatic relation of opposition) can to some extent be ascribed to a construction put upon the phenomena. Even if the premise is entertained, moreover, it still does not follow that binary classification is an accommodation to a dual reality. The emphasis is therefore thrown back on to the organizing power of the mind. This is a factor that Hallpike implicitly admits, and both he and Lloyd actually advance another hypothesis that rests in effect on a supposed propensity of thought.

Hallpike remarks in passing (1979:228):

> it is undoubtedly true that people at all levels of mental development have a propensity to *reduce* complex situations to binary relations and that comparison in particular seems to be facilitated by the consideration of elements two at a time; but this does not justify the contention that binary *classification* is simply an expression of a dualistic propensity of the human mind.

The generalizations advanced here are of much consequence as possible grounds of binary classification, and Hallpike's command of the psychological literature is such as to encourage us to accept them. Whether it should be proposed that binary classification is "simply" the result of a dualistic propensity is another question, and not a simple one in itself. Hallpike returns to the matter of simplicity on a subsequent page where he concludes that we may expect to find pairs of items, in all the variety he has described, conventionally associated in the collective representations of all cultures. He restates the proposition that differentiation and comparison are fundamental, both at the perceptual and at the conceptual levels of mental functioning, and then he adds: "the division of, or grouping of, things into pairs is the simplest form of differentiation and comparison" (p. 233). He does not explicitly say as much, and indeed he does not expatiate at all on this issue, but the implication seems to be that the very simplicity of an assortment into pairs is an additional factor contributing to the development of binary classification.

The emphasis on simplicity appears in Lloyd's argument as well. In discussing theories based on opposites in early Greek thought, he writes: "If we ask why *opposites* are referred to especially frequently in different contexts in such doctrines, one fairly obvious suggestion that we may make is that opposites provide simple and distinct reference points to which other things may be related" (1966:65). In cosmology, physics, and biology, as well as in ethics and politics, "part of the attraction of opposite principles lies, no doubt, in their abstract clarity and their apparent comprehensiveness"; to refer to a pair or to pairs of opposite principles "has obvious advantages in terms of clarity and economy" (p. 66).

In the latter part of his survey, Lloyd returns to a comparative viewpoint, and he observes that "many factors" appear to contribute to "the remarkable prevalence of theories based on opposites" in so many societies at different stages of technological development. First among these factors, he says, is the fact that many prominent phenomena in nature exhibit a certain duality. Secondly, the duality of nature often acquires an added significance as the symbolic manifestation of fundamental religious or spiritual categories. And then there is a third factor: that opposites provide "a simple framework of reference" by means of which complex phenomena of all sorts may be described or classified. Lloyd concludes, in this connection: "Antithesis is an element in any classification, and the primary form of antithesis, one may say, is division into *two* groups—so that the *simplest* form of classification, by the same token, is a dualist one" (p. 80).

This last contention has in its turn a predecessor. A structural analysis of a system of prescriptive alliance among the Aimol of the Indo-Burma border concludes with a theoretical summary on the topic of dualism as a natural and perhaps logically necessary mode of thought. The common feature of various dualistic representations, it is proposed, is not simply duality but the relation of opposition between the terms. "In order to think at all we must distinguish, and . . . the simplest form of distinction is opposition. It is this simple logical fact . . . which is the ground for the universality of dualistic schemes of classification" (Needham 1960b : 104).

The factor of sheer simplicity, as one explanation for the prevalence of binary classification, has thus found at least three apparently independent proponents in recent years. But all three theorists can be seen as reiterating a more fundamental point made in 1787 by Kant: "all *a priori* division of concepts must be by dichotomy" (1964:116). This is a formulation of capital importance, for it does not rest on tacit criteria of simplicity or economy but on the *a priori* nature of dualism as a mode of classification. Indeed, this must be the only *a priori* mode, for as soon as a triadic partition is contemplated there necessarily intervenes some stipulation that is not contained in the elementary operation of dichotomy. By this account, dichotomy is the formal paradigm of the pure concept of classification.

Nevertheless, the causal connection between the utter simplicity of dichotomy and the elaboration of dual classification by resort to opposites remains unexplained. Evidently there is a formal similarity between the two, namely that dichotomy is a paradigm of dual classification whereas the classification can be seen as its systematic expression, so that both are instances of duality. But this common feature does not justify the inference that dual classification owes its global distribution to the simplicity of a partition into two. The hidden premise behind this idea is that what is simple will be adopted because it is simple, but there is no evident proof that this is correct. Moreover, the premise can be variously formulated according to the mode of causation that it assumes, and the supposed advantages of the simple over the complex will vary accordingly.

If we consider the generalizations mentioned by Hallpike, under this aspect, the results are equivocal. One proposition is that people tend to reduce complex situations to binary relations, so that dual classifications can be seen as products of a general mental endeavor in the direction of the simple. But this explanation stands in contrast with the hypothesis that such classifications embody the "primary" form of antithesis. What seems to be implied by the latter proposition, as also by the assertion that dual classification is grounded in opposition as the simplest form of distinction, is that classificatory thought tends to resort initially to dualism. Either of these hypotheses would serve, if it could be proved in a causal sense, as evidence for an inherent property of the mind: either it works toward the simplicity of dualism, or else it starts from dualism by virtue of its simplicity. But in each of these formulations the assumed causation is different, and so is the operation of the postulated tendency toward the simple. The tendency cannot be defined by reference to the structure of representations that are presumed to be its products, but only by identifying the operation by which these representations are formed. Granted that simplicity is the product, still we cannot say that it expresses a particular proclivity until the mode of causation has been isolated.

The other proposition adduced by Hallpike is that comparison seems to be facilitated by the comparison of elements two at a time. This may well be so, but it has no direct bearing on the analysis of dual symbolic classification. There is no evidence that such classification is a product of detached comparison for the sake of any particular purpose, and so far as the evidences go it is decidedly not the function of systems of the kind to effect comparison (Needham 1980:58). If a simplification is at work, therefore, it is almost certainly not in the service of comparison. The function of dualism is the provision of a conceptual order, not to make contingent comparative statements about dyads or their constituent terms. If it does not facilitate comparison in its actual employment, there is no compulsion to think that such a supposed advantage was a factor in the development of dual classification. In any case, dual classification does not consist in the mere accumulation of elements two at a time, but it is systematic. When we examine the constitution of such a system, it is a question wherein the postulated simplicity is supposed to be found.

VIII

An unqualified duality is certainly simple, but a system of dual classification cannot be constructed by means of the principle of duality alone. In fact, two other principles—analogy and homology—are also implicated, as depicted in figure 6 (after Needham 1980:47, fig. 1).

This figure, drawn in order to demonstrate the quaternary structure of analogy, serves to bring out the main features of a system of dual classification. There are two dyads, A/B and C/D. They are connected into a system

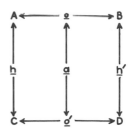

Figure 6. Quaternary Structure of Analogy

by the proportional analogy A : B :: C : D. The three constituent principles are opposition (*o*), analogy (*a*), and homology (*h*). These stand in an order of logical priority: first opposition, then analogy, and subsequently homology. Together, they compose a systematic resource that can be seen as the module with which a scheme of dual classification is constructed, for example that of the Meru (table 7). The basic relation is dual, and it is this that is supposed to ground the simplicity of the system.

Taken as it stands, this formal representation is indeed relatively simple. It consists of only four terms, and these are coherently interrelated by just three principles. But when we consider what is implicit in this representation the impression of simplicity soon recedes. Some of the main complications have already been isolated in *Reconnaissances* (Needham 1980, chap. 2), but for the present purpose there is still occasion for an independent review of certain features of the system.

Let us begin with the dyads, taking as example A/B. These two terms can be like or unlike. If it is found a hindrance that like terms should be represented by unlike letters, let it be stipulated that the letters A–D composing the quadrate shall stand for loci, not entities. The terms can be of equal or unequal value, and in the latter case the relationship can be qualified either as A>B or as A<B. On this point it may be stressed that we are dealing with a formal construction, and that whether the terms are valued alike or differently is equally possible from a formal point of view.

Empirically, however, Beck is correct when she writes: "It is difficult to find any conceptual antithesis which is truly symmetric except in a formal sense. Nearly all such oppositions have some evaluative connotation implying a superior-inferior relationship" (1973:421 n. 15). There can apparently be exceptions, as with the pairs hot/cold and dry/wet in early Greek philosophy, of which Lloyd writes that "there is nothing to suggest that one of each pair is thought of as in any way superior to the other" (1966: 56–57). But Aristotle held that right, above, and front were "*more honourable* than their opposites" (p. 52); and certain Greek philosophers "first explicitly formulated the distinction in *value* between the opposite terms of certain pairs" (p. 62). So far as more modern ethnographic evidence is concerned, "it is indeed commonly found that dyadic terms in a binary system are of unequal value, and that one term is assessed as 'superior' in some respect or another to its opposite" (Needham 1980:57).

Then, if the relationship is such as can have direction (cf. Matilal 1968:31–32), it can be qualified either as A → B or as A ← B. If the terms are glossed as having a propositional content (this is a formal possibility, not a factual postulate; see Needham 1980:51), the relationship can be symmetric or it can be asymmetric; that is, the proposition implicit in A : B is the same as its converse B : A, or else it is not the same (see above, chap. 8, sec. III). Finally, the relationship that is represented as opposition can be analyzed as consisting of at least seven types of relation (see chap. 4; five such are included in table 4), or as thirteen types (chap. 5, sec. V), or as an indeterminate number of types of dyadic relation.

At the limit, indeed, it can be proposed that "there are as many discriminable modes of opposition as there are dyads" (Needham 1980: 55)—on the premise, that is, that each dyad expresses only one mode of opposition, for on the defensible premise that each dyad can express more than one mode the limit must be extended still further, and there will be more modes of opposition exemplified than there are dyads in the system. If it should be objected that this latter proposal carries analysis itself beyond due limits, there are two immediate responses. The first is that on the premise stated the conclusion is valid, and that we have no prior reason to expect any other conclusion. The second response is that there is a close parallel with an actual philosophical doctrine; in the ancient Indian school of philosophy (fl. 13th century) known as Navya-nyāya ("the New Logic") relational abstractions were not treated as universals, in the sense of repeatable forms of an entity, but "they were taken as nonrepeatable particulars peculiar to each occurrence" (Matilal 1968: 33).

On these various grounds, therefore, and according to the criteria that to some extent have to be selected by the analyst, it is plain that the relationship constituting a dyad is by no means simple or given. Although there are only two terms related in each instance, the relationship between them has no intrinsic simplicity.

The principle of analogy, next, is rather more difficult to deal with, within the scope of the present investigation, for the reason that the analysis of analogy as a discrete relation has not been taken very far, either formally or in the study of ordinary discourse. Some of the main features of its em-

pirical employment as a nonhierarchic mode of classification have been outlined elsewhere (Needham 1980, chap. 2),
but the intricacy that can be glimpsed in the use of analogy
has not yet been explicated. Nevertheless, enough is understood to permit some test of the idea that analogy, as a
principle in dual classification, contributes to the supposed
simplicity of such systems.

The view that the relation between dyads is analogical is
clearly stated by Lloyd, and it is a relation that is characteristic of the philosophies of Heraclitus and the Pythagoreans.
Their doctrines "depend on the recognition of an *analogy*
or *equivalence* between the relationships between pairs of
opposites of many different sorts" (1966:99; cf. 96). The
notion of equivalence may seem to imply that the relation
of analogy between dyads is alike from one instance to another, or perhaps that there is even an identical mode of relation. Formally speaking, again, the figure does permit
that inference, and then the relation will be taken as simple.
But when we take into account any of the sources of differentiation that affect relationships within dyads, it must follow that the analogical relationship will reflect that complexity. It is only when the terms of each dyad happen to
be identically related, by all the formal criteria that we have
surveyed above, that the analogy between the dyads will
match the simplicity of the figure, but this is no more than
a purely formal hypothesis. If we admit in addition the factor of semantic differentiation (cf. Needham 1980:54), the
relationship will appear as even more complex than are the
intricate permutations produced by the formal criteria.

In sum, then, if we consider the relationships in a system
of dual classification as social facts, the instances of opposition that are analogically linked can be regarded as composing what Vygotsky called a "chain complex" (Needham

1980:62). This means that, in what Lloyd aptly describes as the "recurrent antithesis" by which a table of opposites is built up (1966:41), there is no constant relation of analogy such as could be called simple.

The principle of homology has not yet received much in the way of formal attention, but comparative analysis has led to the generalization that homologues are "remarkably disparate" (Needham 1980:56). This is, of course, a consequence of the fact that the dyads themselves are highly various, both formally and semantically. Despite the simplicity of our figure, therefore, it will not be expected by now that the instances of the principle of homology will be simple in any sense.

The conclusion to our summary review of the constituent principles of dual classification is thus that in their empirical expression they are various and complex. By contrast, we have to look on a scheme such as that in figure 6 as a purely formal construction, or else as a highly abstract representation of the characteristic features of dual classification. Under each of these aspects a system based on opposites can well give the appearance of being simple, and the inference is thereby encouraged that it directly reflects the postulated simplicity of the act of mind responsible for "the primary form of antithesis" or "the simplest form of distinction." Hence we are led to ascribe to the causation of systems of dual classification a simplicity which as collective representations they do not possess; and conversely we are led to infer from the simple construction by which these systems can be represented that the corresponding properties of thought and imagery are equally simple. It is possible to suggest that the formal simplicity actually is matched by correspondingly simple mental processes, but that when they are operationalized as social phenomena they are subject to differentiation and complication such as ideal constructs of other kinds commonly undergo. This hypothesis is a possibility but it is purely speculative; it not testable either by analysis or by observation. The postulated simplicity cannot be salvaged by this means.

Finally there is yet another kind of objection to the formulation that we have been examining. Dichotomy has been taken as absolutely simple, and in particular as the simplest possible mode of classification, but this latter premise can be resisted. Ogden, in contending that serial order is easier to determine than is hierarchical order, states: "the mechanism of the Scale and the Cut is less intricate than that of Dichotomy and the Porphyrian tree" (1967:19; see above, chap. 5). His reasons for thinking so are that the former distinctions are constantly employed in everyday affairs, whereas very few philosophers could dichotomize "Inventions." The cogency of this particular argument, as it might be fully worked out, is not immediately self-evident, but that is not the present point. The real impact of this proposal is that it is not patently self-contradictory or otherwise absurd, so that dichotomy can seriously be considered less simple than some other method. If it is not the simplest conceivable mode of distinction or classification, then it loses its status as the axiomatic premise to the formulations in question. Another challenge to the premise is posed by Blanché, who argues that a graduated scale is an intrinsically simpler structure than an "oppositional structure" (1966:17). Here, too, the ultimate cogency of this contention is secondary to the appreciation that opposition can logically be considered less simple than another method of distinction or classification. Once again, therefore, the very criterion of basic simplicity has been called into real question, and so therefore must be the hypotheses that derive dual classification from it.

It should be remarked, nevertheless, that none of these considerations invalidates figure 6 as a theoretical scheme. It is composed of abstractions drawn inductively from the comparative analysis of systems of dual symbolic classification. If the interpretation of each term and each relation has to be variously qualified, in reference to the actuality of social facts or of processes of thought, this is no more than we should expect of the degree to which a model corresponds to reality. An abstraction, by definition, does not replicate the concrete particulars of that to which it refers. If the relation of opposition, in particular, can be shown to subsume numerous dual modes that are not reducible one to another, let alone to a common logical form, this fact does not impair the proven utility of the theoretical scheme as a formal construction. The utility of this systematic concept has been demonstrated, it can be maintained, in the determination of the characteristic features of dual symbolic classification (*Right & Left,* introduction) and in the isolation of analogical classification as distinct from hierarchical classification (Needham 1980, chap. 2), as well as in numerous empirical analyses of social facts and philosophical theories that can be represented by tables of opposites (Lloyd 1966).

Yet at the same time it should be reiterated that none of these exercises validates the claim of opposition to be accepted as a distinct and unitary mode of relation. In contrast to the simplicity and economy of the theoretical scheme, this concept has been shown all the more decisively to be in practice an odd-job notion seductively masked by the immediacy of a spatial metaphor.

IX

There is a great contrast between the proliferating conceptual difficulties that we have encountered and what is after all a universal tendency to represent things by twos. Likewise, there is a marked disparity between the formal simplicity of this operation and the numerous complexities that are implicit in dual classification. Certain lines of inquiry immediately follow from these summations. We shall not trace them out here, for although they are premised on the understanding of opposition at which we have arrived, they are problems of a different order. But some of them may well be mentioned, if only because their formulation is promoted by the more perspicuous view of opposition that we now have.

One problem was posed by Hocart in 1936, in connection with the modes of thought underlying dual organization. He considered the question whether dichotomy was traditional or else innate; whether it was merely an old habit that persisted or was something that lay deeper in human nature. He concluded: "perhaps it is a law of nature, but that is not sufficient to explain the dual organization, for dichotomy need not produce a pair, except fleetingly as a first step" (1970:289–90). On the former count, the problem can be rephrased: there is "a nagging doubt concerning the possibility of an innate proclivity of the mind which stops dead as soon as it has achieved an institutionalized form" (editor's introduction, p. lxxxviii). There are certain aspects under which this is a real problem, but we can now see that in one respect at least the gloss is not correctly phrased. It seems an obvious construction to put on the case so long as opposition, or the operation of dichotomy, is conceived as a simple unity; but once this view is given up it is not so plain that the mind does stop dead. The principle may well be retained, but the array of discriminations that it provides for, in one semantic field after another, is indeterminate. Rather than stopping dead, the mind (that is, whatever system of agencies is responsible for dual classification) can be imagined as progressively exploiting the uses to which the principle can be put. There seem indeed to be limits to this kind of development, even in such a comprehensive system as that of the Nyoro (*Right & Left,* chap. 15), and it is possible to suggest certain factors that tend to set these limits (Needham 1980: 59–60), but they do not correspond to the idea that the production of pairs is no more than a transitory and preliminary result of dichotomy.

Another problem has to do with the way in which dual classification is transcended. Waismann has stressed the failure of the Greeks to understand change, by reason of their commitment to polar terms (1968: 178) which they conceived as distinct substances (cf. Lloyd 1966: 81 n. 1). But in the "functional thinking" of science, the idiom of which Waismann dates to the fourteenth century, a language came into use in which such contrasted terms are looked upon as degrees of one and the same quality. "The construction of modern science is bound up with it and would not have been possible without it" (p. 179). It is a change from a static to a dynamic view, and concomitantly a change from contrastive representation in terms of opposites to relative estimation by reference to a scale. As Blanché phrases the matter, modern science was born from the "decision" to treat quality as a dimension; in place of irresoluble oppositions there was substituted a graduated scale that was to permit the interrelation of qualities hitherto taken to be heterogeneous. "The oppositional structure thus appears to have been banished from scientific thought" (1966:16–17). In the event, however, the use of metrical scales was added to that of oppositional schemes without abolishing them (p. 18). Hence there coexist in scientific research two types of problems, reflecting two types of structures: graduated and oppositional (p. 19). The resort to opposites has therefore not been entirely superseded (cf. Waismann 1968:179–80); but the realization of the possibility of transcending opposites, in favor of the dimensional scale, is nevertheless one of the most momentous developments in the history of thought. How exactly this transformation came about is highly problematical, but one thing at least is quite sure: the problem cannot be correctly formulated unless the structure of classification by opposites is first clearly understood. In this intellectual venture, the analysis of the concept of opposition is basic and crucial.

It is not only in the technical deconstruction of systems of dual classification, or in the historical reconstruction of the development of scientific thought, that there are consequential problems about opposition. Another domain is that of the imagination, and this is theoretically important because it tends to show that the impulsion behind opposition is not solely logical or classificatory, and because it tends also to confirm that opposites can be the products of subliminal factors. Steinberg's drawing (frontispiece) has provided us with initial evidence for this case. Armstrong has argued that the foundation of Shakespeare's imaginative thought was the realization of a dualism in life; "his mind was dominated by the warring opposites disclosed by experience" (1946:93). More generally, Bachelard contends that "true images, the images of rêverie, are unitary or binary"; the mixing of the elements (water, earth, fire, air) by the material imagination has a "dualistic character" (1942:129; cf. Needham 1985, chap. 1). The sphere of representational art of all kinds is also replete with examples of dyadic contrasts such as are commonly referred to as opposites, and this is true of India and China and of hundreds of less articulate civilizations such as those of the Northwest Coast or the Sepik. The great range within which products of the imagination are organized by opposition works to strengthen the inference that in other semantic fields as well a like influence, below the threshold of conscious appreciation or deliberation, is ultimately responsible.

X

We have commented repeatedly on the parts played, in theories about opposition, by reificatory terms of exposition and by the spatial metaphor of opposition.

No doubt the reification is in part at least the product of a very common tendency to represent mental processes and qualities by means of images and expressions taken from mechanical operations and material objects (see Needham 1983, chap. 4). Naturally there is a spatial aspect to this tendency, for the objects referred to are three-dimensional and have locations; but in the present instance it is the source of the spatial metaphor, constituting the very designations of the mode of relation (opposition, antithesis, counterpoint), that calls for renewed attention. The linguistic evidences that we have collated (above, chap. 3, sec. II) seem to point to a quasi-universal apperception that is registered in remarkably similar ways with reference to relative positions in space. It is a persuasive inference that this extensive range of like expressions has its origin in a spatial intuition. To adduce the factor of intuition is not to resort to some occult faculty or inaccessible means of cognition. We can take the idea of intuition to stand for "that representation which can be given prior to all thought" (Kant 1964:153). In this sense we are dealing with a mode of apperception that is by definition subliminal and hence obscure; but at the same time it is something with which we are familiarized, significantly, by our body image. A sustainable conclusion, which can be reached both by induction and by elimination, is that subtending the complexities of dual representations there is a vectorial mode of spatial intuition.

By this account, we are not dealing fundamentally with a logical imperative or a cognitive necessity, nor with a highly general relational abstraction that is a common component in ratiocination (see chap. 3, sec. III), but with a nonconceptual apprehension. The present investigation thus provides another argument against intellectualism; that is, against the "presumption that in the study of social facts, and more generally in the interpretation of human experience, intellectual considerations must be preponderant or even decisive" (Needham 1978:51). It provides a further demonstration that our task is to come to terms, as nearly as we can, with "the intrinsic properties of social facts," and also that intellectualism can powerfully prevent our doing so (p. 53). It has certainly got in the way of a perspicuous view of the concept of opposition, which, despite the typology of Aristotle and the rectifications by Lloyd, has commonly been treated as though it were a unitary relation with distinct logical properties. There is some justification to think that classification by binary opposition is "an elementary and universal mode of classification," even if we have to adduce many sorts of qualification when we address any individual instance, but there is no good reason to accept that opposition is intrinsically a "simple relation" (cf. Needham 1979:32).

A consequence of all this is that the comparative analysis of social facts has once more been made yet more difficult, in that what had been thought straightforward has turned out to be very intricate, so that the number of variables to be correlated is very much increased. But at the same time our comprehension has been advanced, for we have identified some of the main causes of our mistakes about opposition. Prominent among these is a "craving for generality" (Wittgenstein 1958:18), combined with the common inclination that the existence of a substantive "makes us look for a thing that corresponds to it" (p. 1)—indeed, as in the present case, to presume that it must exist. A critique of the latter influence can work in opposite directions: in the case of the concept of "belief," the conclusion is that there is no such entity, in the form of a distinct inner state (Needham 1972); in the case of the concept of "opposition," the conclusion is that there are altogether too many types of relation answering to the substantive, and that none of them constitutes the proper and absolute sense of the concept.

The appreciation of this fact about opposition is hindered by another factor: that there is a tendency to slip into treating diagrams as the actual objects of comprehension, as though they were concrete replicas of social facts (Needham 1983:17). Hence it is possible to treat the connections in a diagram such as figure 6 as though they were simple relations, rather than as abstract representations of complex social facts, and thereby to impute to the ethnographic evidence properties that it does not possess. Similarly, it is apparently possible to regard a table of opposites as constituting a concrete entity (chap. 8, sec. II; cf. chap. 2), and thereby to attribute to it various uses that it cannot possess. In each of these two examples it is necessary instead to see the diagram for what it is, namely a graphic articulation of abstractions, and then to "look through" these at the phenomena with which they are tenuously connected.

Finally, in this summary catalogue of mistakes, there is of course the tendency to reificatory thought, and also the treatment of the spatial metaphor of opposition as though it were homogeneous with intrinsic attributes of the concept. In the light of these subversive factors, it is not wholly surprising that the concept should have been so badly misconstrued—and of course it is in any case far easier to consider opposition as a unitary, discrete, simple, and necessary relation. This view of opposition may be a compound mistake, but it has many attractions, including the suasion of the metaphor; and, "naturally, a plausible error finds less resistance in the world than the truth" (Lichtenberg 1971 : 564).

If in the end it is asked what is the positive outcome of the present investigation, one answer is that it consists of every point of argument or analysis that has been settled, one way or the other, throughout the examination of the case for opposition. If it is asked, more narrowly, what is the correct meaning of "opposition," the answer is that the question is misdirected. There is no attribute of opposition that is both essential and distinctive. In contrast with truly formal concepts, such as symmetry or transitivity, opposition has no intrinsic logical form. There is no proper definition, but instead only an indefinite aggregate of various dyadic relations holding between variables of many disparate kinds. The modes of opposition make up a polythetic class of contrasts.

The characteristic features (see Needham 1972 : 120–21)

of the members of this class are that they are dyadic and that they are designated by spatial metaphors. The ground of these metaphors, and perhaps one explanation of their impress, may be a spatial intuition. This inferred mode of apperception, reflecting perhaps a cerebrational vector (see Needham 1981:25, 87), is registered in language and is diversified in collective representations; these representations, at the limit of development, are conjoined into systems of dual classification. But the proclivity of which the systems are end-products is a directive, not a blueprint; it forms a module in the architectonics of thought and imagery, but it is not a semantic constructor. As Hallpike enlighteningly observes, what gives meaning to symbolic oppositions is a vast range of implicit knowledge common to the culture of a people, and "these categories are related by a complex set of associations which are not reducible to dualistic form" (1979:232–33). The circumstantial nature of this ideological ambience helps us to understand the indeterminacy of individual dyads, and hence how it is that the supposed relation of opposition evades a strict identification.

There is a quizzical exchange in *Waiting for Godot* (Beckett 1956:21) that will serve as epitome. Estragon has been eating a carrot; he raises what remains by the stub of leaf, twirls it before his eyes, and remarks that the more you eat the worse it gets. Vladimir replies that with him it is "just the opposite." Asked to explain, he says that he gets used to the muck as he goes along. Then,

ESTRAGON (*after prolonged reflection*): "Is that the opposite?"
VLADIMIR: "Question of temperament."

Bibliography

Ackrill, J. L.
    1963   *See* Aristotle.

Aristotle
    1961   *Metaphysics.* Ed. and trans. John Warrington. London: Dent; New York: Dutton.
    1963   *Categories and De Interpretatione.* Trans., notes J. L. Ackrill. Oxford: At the Clarendon Press.

Armstrong, Edward A.
    1946   *Shakespeare's Imagination: A Study of the Psychology of Association and Inspiration.* London: Lindsay Drummond.

Ayer, A. J.
    1954   *Philosophical Essays.* London: Macmillan; New York: St. Martin's Press.

Bachelard, Gaston
    1942   *L'Eau et les rêves: essai sur l'imagination de la matière.* Paris: José Corti.

Bateson, Gregory
    1936   *Naven: A Survey of the Problems Suggested by a Composite Picture of the Culture of a New Guinea Tribe Drawn from Three Points of View.* Cambridge: At the University Press.
    1958   *Naven.* Second ed. Stanford: Stanford University Press.

Beck, Brenda E. F.
    1973   "The Right-Left Division of South Indian Society." In Needham, ed.: 391–426.

Bibliography

Beckett, Samuel
   1956   *Waiting for Godot: A Tragicomedy in Three Acts.* London: Faber and Faber.
Beidelman, T. O.
   1973   "Kaguru Symbolic Classification." In Needham, ed.: 128–66.
Benveniste, Emile
   1966   *Problèmes de linguistique générale.* Paris: Gallimard.
Bernardi, Bernardo
   1959   *The Mugwe, A Failing Prophet: A Study of a Religious and Public Dignitary of the Meru of Kenya.* London: Oxford University Press for the International African Institute.
   1971   "Il Mugwe dei Meru (Kenya): da istituzione sociale a valore culturale." *Africa: Rivista trimestrale di Studi e Documentazione dell'Istituto Italiano per l'Africa* 26: 427–42. Rome.
   1983   *Il Mugwe: Un Profeta che Scompare.* Milan: Franco Angeli.
Blanché, Robert
   1966   *Structures intellectuelles: essai sur l'organisation systématique des concepts.* Pref. Georges Davy. Paris: J. Vrin.
Borges, Jorge Luis
   1968   *Other Inquisitions 1937–52.* Trans. Ruth L. C. Simms. New York: Simon and Schuster.
Browne, Thomas
   1643   *Religio Medici.* London.
   1646   *Pseudodoxia Epidemica.* London.
   1716   *Christian Morals.* London.
Calvino, Italo
   1955   *Le Vicomte pourfendu (Il Visconte dimezzato).* Trans. Juliette Bertrand. Paris: Albin Michel.
Cassirer, Ernst
   1953–57   *The Philosophy of Symbolic Forms.* Trans. Ralph Manheim. 3 vols. New Haven and London: Yale University Press.
Dauzat, Albert, et al.
   1964   *Nouveau dictionnaire étymologique et historique.* Paris: Librairie Larousse.

Bibliography

Delfendahl, Bernard
1973 *Le Clair et l'obscur*. Paris: Editions Anthropos.
Dumont, Louis
1978 "La Communauté anthropologique et l'idéologie." *L'Homme* 18:83–110.
1982 "On Value." Radcliffe-Brown Lecture 1980. *Proceedings of the British Academy* 66 (1980):207–41.
1983 *Essais sur l'individualisme: une perspective anthropologique sur l'idéologie moderne*. Paris: Éditions du Seuil.
Durkheim, Emile, and Mauss, Marcel
1963 *Primitive Classification*. Trans. and ed. with intr. Rodney Needham. Chicago: University of Chicago Press.
Erman, Adolf, and Grapow, Hermann
1925–50 *Wörterbuch der aegyptischen Sprache*. 6 vols. Leipzig: J. C. Hinrich.
Fadiman, Jeffrey
1973 "Early History of the Meru of Mount Kenya." *Journal of African History* 14:9–27.
1976 *Mountain Warriors: The Pre-colonial Meru of Kenya*. Papers in International Studies, African Series 27. Athens, Ohio: Ohio University Center for International Studies.
Fischer, Ludwig
1931 *The Structure of Thought: A Survey of Natural Philosophy*. Trans. W. H. Johnston. London: George Allen & Unwin.
Grebe, Paul, ed.
1963 *Etymologie: Herkunftswörterbuch der deutschen Sprache*. Der Grosse Duden 7. Mannheim: Bibliographisches Institut.
Hallpike, C. R.
1979 *The Foundations of Primitive Thought*. Oxford: Clarendon Press.
Hertz, Robert
1909 "Le Prééminence de la main droite: étude sur la polarité religieuse." *Revue philosophique* 68:553–80.
1973 "The Pre-eminence of the Right Hand: A Study in Religious Polarity." In Needham, ed.:3–31.

Bibliography

Hocart, A. M.

1970 *Kings and Councillors: An Essay in the Comparative Anatomy of Human Society.* Ed. and intr. Rodney Needham; pref. E. E. Evans-Pritchard. Chicago and London: University of Chicago Press. (First ed., Cairo, 1936.)

Jacobson-Widding, Anita

1979 *Red-White-Black as a Mode of Thought.* Uppsala Studies in Cultural Anthropology 1. Stockholm: Almquist & Wiksell International.

Kant, Immanuel

1964 *Critique of Pure Reason.* Trans. Norman Kemp Smith. London: Macmillan; New York: St. Martin's Press.

Karlgren, Bernhard

1923 *Analytic Dictionary of Chinese and Sino-Japanese.* Paris: Geuthner. Repr., New York: Dover Publications, 1974.

1964 *Grammata Serica Recensa.* Göteborg: Elanders Boktryckeri.

Korn, Francis

1973 *Elementary Structures Reconsidered: Lévi-Strauss on Kinship.* London: Tavistock Publications; Berkeley: University of California Press.

Lalande, André, ed.

1951 *Vocabulaire technique et critique de la philosophie.* Sixth ed. Paris: Presses Universitaires de France.

Laughton, W. H.

1944 *The Meru.* The Peoples of Kenya 10. Nairobi: Ndia Kuu Press.

Lichtenberg, Georg Christoph

1968 *Schriften und Briefe, 1: Sudelbücher.* Ed. Wolfgang Promies. Munich: Carl Hanser.

1971 *Schriften und Briefe, 2: Sudelbücher II, Materialhefte, Tagebücher.* Ed. Wolfgang Promies. Munich: Carl Hanser.

Littlejohn, James

1973 "Temne Right and Left: An Essay on the Choreography of Everyday Life." In Needham, ed.: 288–98.

Littré, Emile

1963 *Dictionnaire de la langue française.* Abbr. A. Beaujean. Paris: Editions Universitaires.

Bibliography

Lloyd, G. E. R.
1966 *Polarity and Analogy: Two Types of Argumentation in Early Greek Thought.* Cambridge: At the University Press.
1973 "Right and Left in Greek Philosophy." In Needham, ed.: 167–86.

Mahner, Jurg
1975 "The Outsider and the Insider in Tigania Meru." *Africa* 45: 400–9.

Matilal, Bimal Krishna
1968 *The Navya-nyāya Doctrine of Negation.* Harvard Oriental Studies 46. Cambridge, Mass.: Harvard University Press.

Morel, Bernard
1962 *Dialectiques du mystère.* Pref. Stéphane Lupasco. Paris: La Colombe.

Morris, Marshall
1981 *Saying and Meaning in Puerto Rico: Some Problems in the Ethnography of Discourse.* Oxford: Pergamon Press.

Needham, Rodney
1960a "The Left Hand of the Mugwe: An Analytical Note on the Structure of Meru Symbolism." *Africa* 30: 20–33. Repr. in Needham, ed. 1973: 109–27; trans. B. Bernardi as "La Mano sinistra del Mugwe," appx. II in Bernardi 1983: 193–209.
1960b "A Structural Analysis of Aimol Society." *Bijdragen tot de Taal-, Land- en Volkenkunde* 116: 81–108.
1972 *Belief, Language, and Experience.* Oxford: Basil Blackwell; Chicago: University of Chicago Press.
1973 ed., *Right & Left: Essays on Dual Symbolic Classification.* Chicago and London: University of Chicago Press.
1974 *Remarks and Inventions: Skeptical Essays about Kinship.* London: Tavistock Publications; New York: Harper & Row.
1978 *Primordial Characters.* Charlottesville: University Press of Virginia. (Paperback repr., corr., 1985.)
1979 *Symbolic Classification.* Santa Monica: Goodyear Publishing; distributed by Random House, New York.
1980 *Reconnaissances.* Toronto: University of Toronto Press.

1981   *Circumstantial Deliveries.* Quantum Books. Berkeley, Los Angeles, and London: University of California Press.

1983   *Against the Tranquility of Axioms.* Berkeley, Los Angeles, and London: University of California Press.

1985   *Exemplars.* Berkeley, Los Angeles, and London: University of California Press.

Ogden, C. K.

1932   *Opposition: A Linguistic and Psychological Analysis.* London: Kegan Paul, Trench, Trubner.

1967   *Opposition: A Linguistic and Psychological Analysis.* Intr. I. A. Richards. Bloomington: Indiana University Press.

Onions, C. T.

1966   *The Oxford Dictionary of English Etymology.* Oxford: At the Clarendon Press.

Robert, Paul

1966   *Dictionnaire . . . de la langue française,* vol. 3. Paris.

Rosenberg, Harold

1978   *Saul Steinberg.* New York: Alfred A. Knopf.

Simon, W.

1947   *Chinese-English Dictionary.* London: Lund Humphries.

Steinberg, Saul

1965   *The New World.* London: Hamish Hamilton.

Swedenborg, Emanuel

1955   "Correspondences and Representations." In *Psychological Transactions,* trans. and ed. Alfred Acton: 215–61. Philadelphia: Swedenborg Scientific Association.

Tarde, Gabriel de

1897   *L'Opposition universelle: essai d'une théorie des contraires.* Paris: Félix Alcan.

Tcherkézoff, Serge

1983   *Le Roi nyamwezi, la droite et la gauche.* Cambridge: Cambridge University Press; Paris: Editions de la Maison des Sciences de l'Homme. English edition forthcoming from Cambridge University Press.

Trésor . . .

1981   *Trésor de la langue française,* vol. 9. Paris: Editions du C.N.R.S.

Waismann, F.
  1968   *How I See Philosophy.* Ed. R. Harré. London: Mac-
         millan; New York: St. Martin's Press.
Warrington, John
  1961   *See* Aristotle.
Whitehead, Alfred North
  1958   *The Function of Reason.* Boston: Beacon Press. First
         ed., Princeton University Press, 1929.
Wittgenstein, Ludwig
  1958   *The Blue and Brown Books.* Oxford: Basil Blackwell.
  1967   *Zettel.* Ed. G. E. M. Anscombe and G. H. von Wright;
         trans. G. E. M. Anscombe. Oxford: Basil Blackwell.
  1969   *On Certainty.* Ed. G. E. M. Anscombe and G. H. von
         Wright; trans. Denis Paul and G. E. M. Anscombe.
         Oxford: Basil Blackwell.

Index

245

Index

Index

247

Index

Index

Index

Index

Designer: Kaelin Chappell
Compositor: G&S Typesetters, Inc.
Text: 11/13 Bembo
Display: Bembo
Printer: McNaughton & Gunn, Inc.
Binder: John H. Dekker and Sons